SPIRIT SKILLS
A THINK AND DO BOOK

BY NANCY DOBSON

D1445871

Spirit Skills, a think and do book
By Nancy Dobson, copyright 2018
P.O. Box 71132, Bethesda, Maryland 20813

Library of Congress TXu2-111-812
November 5, 2018

Other books by Nancy Dobson -- In print:

99 Lyrics By Nancy Dobson

SOUL Question

The Gospel's Message Within The Message

The Torah Conscious Christian, Biblical Law by Subject, Paraphrased, With Commentary

The Torah Conscious Christian's Guide To Holy Days
What The Spirit Sees....

Electronic books on Kindle:

If You Ask Me....

SOUL Question

To order copies key the whole title into Amazon's search window. If the title doesn't come up, add, "by Nancy Dobson."

PREFACE

In previous books I have organized the Biblical Law in subject order and shown how Jesus taught the Law by its intentions. Experimenting with the laws myself has led me to find answers to questions I have had about spiritual nature and our reason for being on Earth.

In this book I begin with the premise that everyone on Earth is here in "time out" because we chose our will over God's will. This is symbolized in the Garden of Eden story in the Bible where we blame a snake for lying to us, when it is really our own willfulness that causes us to choose against God's guidance. This concept is repeated in the myths of various religions. It stands to reason, therefore, that the way back to our original home beyond time and substance is to learn how to daily perceive and choose God's will first in our lives -- to submit to our Creator, Who forever loves us and has waited patiently for our repentance. To learn how to perceive and submit to God's will we must first develop spiritual sensitivity.

Spirit Skills, a think and do book, explains ways to develop spiritual sensitivity for the purpose of being able to perceive and submit to God's will. Each chapter begins with a summary of some of the laws in a single category. Following that, laws themselves are explained using quotes from seven major religious traditions. It is significant that every major religion has discovered and taught these laws of spiritual nature. Each of the twenty laws ends with an experiment designed to validate the law and to help develop spiritual sensitivity.

There are laws that govern material nature and laws that govern spiritual nature. Just as we can discern and define the laws of material nature, we can discern and define laws of spiritual nature. Just as we endanger ourselves and

4

others when we break the laws of material nature, we endanger ourselves and others when we break the laws of spiritual nature.   Therefore, it is to our benefit to learn the laws of both and to live within their limits. The added advantage of learning and using the laws of spiritual nature is that it makes it easier for us to prepare for what comes next after our material life.

I would like to thank Dr. Rev. Joyce Emery for her encouragement and for her suggestions for how to improve the format of this book. Her time and suggestions are most appreciated.

I hope the reader will learn something new, exciting and very useful in these pages. All of life is an opportunity to learn, and the most important thing we can learn is how to prepare for our life as it continues beyond this realm. It is with that intent that I offer the following from my research, experiments and observation.

Wishing you God's blessings and guidance,
Nancy Dobson
July 2019

Introduction

In ancient Greece they asked: "Why should I be moral?" Today, scientists answer: because our thoughts and actions cause chemical changes in our body. Good thoughts and actions -- such as honesty, forgiveness and respect -- strengthen our immune system and make us healthier. Buddhists would offer that immorality causes stress in one's self and in one's society. A functional society requires mutual trust, and since immorality causes distrust it undermines the functioning of society. Hindus might answer that being immoral will cause us to feel empty and desperate.

But like a shadow it can't shake is the companion question: "How do we define what is moral?" Is it just behaviors we have learned over millennia that lead to good results? Religions teach some behaviors as laws. How do the religious know what is a law?

Laws applied to materials and energies cause order and function. Certain laws have been applied to bring about our organized and functional universe, which unfolds according to a single design. But to bring order and function to our social universe we need to apply a different kind of law.

As a material product we have been brought about by the imposition of laws. Yet we are a product that is conscious of itself and that seeks the cause of order, and of laws. Just as we can define the laws that govern material nature and apply them to create many material things for convenience, comfort and safety, we also can define the laws of our spiritual nature and apply them to bring better order and function to ourselves and our relationships.

There are libraries full of books wherein writers have debated whether or not the Intelligent Power that created and applied laws to bring about this universe – a Living Power that we call God – exists. Yet we are not convinced of God's existence by what is written in books. We are really only convinced of God's existence by our own personal experiences. For those who have experienced God's presence, power, communication and guidance, nothing anyone can say can disprove God's reality. They have had a personal experience, whether it is a life-saving premonition, uncanny coincidences, a miracle in a time of need, an answer to prayer, the subtle power of spiritual nudges or something else.

Jesus said that God is Spirit, and we must worship God in spirit and in truth. (John 4:24) What causes us to be self-conscious, and how do we become conscious of our unique type of spirit?

Some anthropologists believe that the reason Homo sapiens beat out other hominin species to become the only hominin species of today may have something to do with our penchant for using symbols. They find evidence for this in prehistoric art and jewelry. Symbols are a universal language. We find them used in ancient art and in early pictographic writing.

Since dreams and visions use symbols, they are considered the language of the spirit. It could be that using symbols to communicate in art strengthens the spirit within us, because we are speaking its language. As a result, Homo sapiens' use of symbols caused their brain to develop differently than other species. Further evidence of this is that from prehistoric times all religions have used symbols in pictures, songs and stories to tell what they have discovered about our invisible spirit.

It is our spiritual desire to constantly improve ourselves and our circumstances that drives us to seek how symbols connect to one another, and this enables us to define the cause and effect order created with invisible laws. Our spiritual compassion for others spurs us to articulate and teach the laws that we discover. So, education -- learning and teaching -- is a law of how our spiritual nature works. Learning and teaching changes us physically and mentally. While many animals learn by copying, only in human societies are cause-seeking and teaching universal.

This sequence – our spiritual sensitivity to symbols that lead us to be able to perceive and define invisible cause and effect laws that govern material nature, and our desire to improve coupled with our compassion to teach what we learn to others – sets the stage for us to consider that there are also cause and effect laws that govern our spiritual nature. It is these fixed laws that govern how our spiritual nature works that define morality.

If you fall off a roof and break your arm your family and friends will go on loving you, but because you acted against a law of material nature you will have a painful experience. The Living Power that created the material and spiritual realms loves us, but if we act against Its fixed laws we still get hurt. Seeking to understand and live by the laws of both material nature and spiritual nature is a way to show love and respect to ourselves -- and to our Creator.

Jesus said that all laws (of spiritual nature) can be summed up in two: 1) God is One, and you must love God with all your heart, mind, soul and strength. 2) The second is like it. You must love your neighbor as yourself and treat all others as you want to be treated. (Matthew 22:34-40) This second law, called the Golden Rule, is taught in some form in every stable civilization. As the law of reciprocity, it was known to ancient Egyptians and was taught in China by Confucius. It is implicit in the teachings of karma, the law of inevitable consequences, found in Hinduism and Buddhism.

It appears in the book of Leviticus in the Bible. Jesus raised it to be equal to the First Law – the law to love God completely -- which is the most important law in Judaism, Christianity and Islam. Almost all of the laws in the Bible and the Qur'an explain how to live by these two laws.

Another law of spiritual nature is loyalty. We wouldn't be here if someone had not been loyal to us when we were helpless infants. Infants that are fed and kept clean but never cuddled or talked to, die. Children need loyal mothering for emotional health as much as they need good food for physical health. We can't live without loyalty. One indication of emotional health is that we crave to be loyal.

In religions around the world, it is taught that we are here because we chose our will over our Creator's will. We came from God but we weren't loyal to God. However, our Creator is loyal and loves us forever. So, our Creator doesn't extinguish those who rebel but simply puts us in "time out" in a place where we can recognize our errors and their repercussions and learn how to return to love and submission to the Living Designer and Creator of laws, materials and dimensions.

Repentance means to confess our errors and change our lifestyle. When we acknowledge that we have not lived the way that develops spiritual sensitivity and change our lifestyle habits to include practices that strengthen us spiritually, we are applying the law of repentance. After his resurrection Jesus told his disciples to teach repentance for the remission of sins to all nations. (Luke 24:47) We can't reverse our self-first attitude and develop the ability to perceive God's ready guidance until we acknowledge we have erred -- and change.

Submission to God is the law we all have broken, and that's the reason the world of time and materiality was created.

Learning how to perceive God's guidance and submit to God on a daily basis – showing love and respect to God – is taught in Judaism and Christianity and is the foundation of Islam. No one returns to God's Place – the spiritual home we came from – until they learn and live this law of our spiritual nature.

As it is said in the Bible and the Qur'an, only the righteous can discern God's guidance. (Deuteronomy 11:26-28, 27:26; Surah 28.50) This is a fourth reason why we should be moral. We are designed to be able to listen with our spirit to God's daily guidance and to choose God's will over our own. However, in order to fulfill that design we have to be righteous. Learning and living the laws that govern our spiritual nature helps us to be righteous so that we may perceive and choose God's will first in our lives and fulfill what we are designed to do. To that end it behooves us to learn the laws that govern our spiritual nature and apply them in our lives.

In *Spirit Skills, a think and do book,* I examine twenty such laws as they have been identified by seven religions that have shaped the largest civilizations of today. I also offer exercises with which the reader can experience the validity of the laws and further develop the spiritual sensitivity he or she needs to fulfill their design.

It turns out that the Greeks' sassy question has an answer, and that by seeking its answer we have discovered who we are, why we are here, and the way back to our spiritual home.

Nancy Dobson, Arlington, Virginia

TABLE OF CONTENTS

Abbreviations used in this book are as follows:

An English Interpretation of the Holy Qur'an with full Arabic text, (S)

Authorized King James Version of the Bible (KJV)

Interlinear Greek-English New Testament, King James Version (G-E)

JPS Hebrew-English Tanakh (T)

The Analects of Confucius (A)

The Holy Bible From the Ancient Eastern Text, George M. Lamsa's Translation from the Aramaic of the Peshitta (P)

The Interpreter's Bible (IB)

The New Jerusalem Bible (TNJB)

The Oxford Annotated Bible, Revised Standard Verson (OAB)

Genesis (GN)
Exodus (EX)
Leviticus (LV)
Numbers (NU)
Deuteronomy (DT)

Matthew (MT)
Mark (MK)
Luke (LK)
John (JN)

All Bible quotes are from the King James Version of the Bible unless otherwise noted.

CHAPTER ONE

LAW,
SPIRITUALITY and
LAWS OF SPIRITUAL NATURE

LAW

If matter had free will and chose to act against the laws that govern material nature, all the universe would be chaos. We have free will, and when we choose to not live by the laws that govern spiritual nature, we cause chaos within ourselves and our relationships. Laws are cause and effect, whether they govern what is material or what is spiritual.

How do we know something is a law? Laws are forces that create order. They are applied to materials in order to bring forth a specific design. Laws applied to materials brought about our universe, including all the vast, intricate, interconnected systems on Earth.

Laws exist independently of us. We can define their cause and effect order, but we can't change the laws themselves. However, we have the freedom to choose whether or not to live by some laws. When we choose them, we enjoy the benefits that are gained from living within their limits. In addition, we also have the ability to discover and verify for ourselves through experimentation the definitions of laws.

Invisible laws can be defined. First, we experience a law. After recognizing and reflecting on our experience, we can experiment with it deliberately and define its cause and effect order. We can devise various experiments to test our hypothesis of what causes a specific effect. When we understand this sequence, others are able to conduct the same experiments and get the same results. After learning some laws, we can recognize their categories and see how they work together to support a design.

Knowing the laws in the categories of mechanics, chemistry, electro magnetism and such helps us understand how the material realm works. Knowing the laws in the categories of accountability, communication, love, respect and spiritual seeking helps us understand how the spiritual realm works. We can use this information for our spiritual benefit, just as we use the laws that govern the material realm for our material benefit.

People in the ancient world were intimately aware of the order in the development of plants and animals, and the progression of lights in the night sky. They planned their lives around them. Similarly, they didn't need to study the Fundamental Laws for social order, because these rules also were obvious to them. Among the 42 Divine Principles of Behavior found in the ancient *Egyptian Book of the Dead* we find the petitioner saying that he/she has not killed men or women, and has not stolen, lied, committed adultery, or been deceitful. It also affirmed that the petitioner exercised self-discipline in obeying the laws and acting with forethought. Even the ancient Egyptians had a form of the Golden Rule. They taught reciprocity – that is, that those who helped others could expect to receive help when they needed it. This shows that they understood that behavior follows cause and effect rules, and that achieving balance through behavior that can be returned in kind keeps peace inside one's self and in society. They also recognized the existence of the spiritual realm and believed that the gods were angry if their rules were broken. Acknowledging that the spiritual realm exists, in itself, implies an awareness that order exists in that realm that causes consequences to follow actions.

No matter how primitive the people, they tended to form groups. Living in groups gives more benefits than living independently. The larger the group, the safer and more comfortable are the people because a large group can repel attackers and their shared work and information helps meet everyday needs and create conveniences. But in order to keep any group of people cooperating and productive, everyone has to follow the same basic rules of behavior. The group won't cohere if it is full of murderers, thieves, liars or disloyal members. These behaviors tear groups of any size apart. So, the Fundamental Laws to not kill, steal or lie, and to avoid certain sexual behaviors and deliberate rule breaking, as well as the principle to treat others as you want to be treated, have been constant in stable civilizations throughout history and are found in religions and secular codes of conduct around the world.

Other laws of spiritual nature, realized through human trial and error, were articulated and formed into religions by those who were especially spiritually sensitive. In every country, while the civil law may be written and enforced, it is the regular reminder to live by the laws that is given in the stories, songs, rituals and exhortations of religions that shapes a law-keeping community.

SPIRITUALITY

From the beginning of recorded history, some people reported experiencing communication with departed loved ones. These experiences convinced them of the reality of the spiritual realm.

The spiritual realm was acknowledged in ancient Egypt, where the nobility prepared for life after physical death. It also was known in India, where it was taught that each person has an eternal spirit that lives on when their material body dies, and that the spirit returns to material life in a new body.

It was because they had experienced spiritual communication that ancient people created gods that they portrayed with statues. They petitioned the statues that represented powers in the spiritual realm to aid them in meeting their needs for safety, health, food and other desires. They wrote songs of praise to them, created festivals to honor them and gave gifts of something valued by the giver to bribe them.

Over time, it developed that tribal chiefs and kings interpreted the gods' communications for the people and created civil laws. The people became weighed down with trying to bribe and appease a multitude of gods who ruled various activities on Earth and who had capricious whims. In addition, the laws the rulers created favored the rich over the poor and changed with each new ruler.

With the exception of Hinduism – which is a group of religions that evolved over thousands of years and that claims no single spiritual leader -- every religion that has shaped a contemporary civilization is the result of a leader whose teachings shattered the status quo and threatened the established rulers of its time.

The group of religions we currently call Hinduism developed piece by piece in India. As religious traditions developed, they began to teach that spirits reincarnate into a pleasant or a punishing life because of spiritual strengths and weaknesses they developed in previous lives. Morality was then stretched to encompass previous unknown behavior as well as future circumstances. People were encouraged to choose moral behavior in their current life in order to avoid punishment in a future life.

After Buddhists began teaching that we may have a last life and escape the cycle of reincarnation, Hindus began teaching that there are Four Paths we may take to reach the goal of spiritual liberation from the cycle of reincarnation. All Four Paths begin with the spiritual cleansing of living by Five Moral Principles.

According to current Hindu teaching, the Eternal Essence of the universe may be referred to as the One, or Absolute, which they call Brahma. Brahma is represented by statues that have separate histories and personalities. The statues are said to be various attributes of Brahma. In temples made for them, the statues are washed and dressed and given praise and sacrifices of food products.

The Buddha ("Enlightened One," also known as Siddhartha Gautama (563-482 B.C.)) struck a blow against India's group of religious traditions by rejecting its caste system, which teaches that people reincarnate into fixed social groups according to their behavior in previous lives. He taught that men and women are equal, and rejected the practice of sati -- widow immolation (which was made illegal in India in 1988). According to this long standing tradition, if a woman's husband died his widow, though living, could be burned to death with him as his body was cremated. The Buddha retained the Indian belief in karma, by which we all receive back the advice and behavior we give to others. He rejected the concept of an All Knowing, All Powerful God. (Nevertheless, in some sects of Buddhism today a realm beyond the material is acknowledged.) The Buddha was especially sensitive to avarice in society. He taught that we can escape avarice and suffering by denying our desires and emotions and by living a very simple and humble life.

The master psychologist, Confucius (K'ung Fu-tzy (551-479 B.C.)) turned Chinese society on its head by defining nobility according to virtues, instead of wealth or heritage. Knowing that most people like to think of themselves as noble, he thereby encouraged everyone to aspire to live virtuously. Though he claimed that he was opposed to laws, his interpretation of virtue embraces the Fundamental Laws and much more, reflecting a deep understanding of human nature and social interaction.

Abraham (born 2247 B.C.(?)) astounded his idol worshipping contemporaries by bowing to the will of a Single, Invisible,

Living God. While other ancient people tried to bribe their gods to do their will, Abraham chose to listen for guidance from the One Invisible Creator of Heaven and Earth and to do the will of that Living Spirit. He listened to God, then moved to Shechem. He listened to God, then chose circumcision. He listened to God, then prepared to sacrifice his youngest son. Abraham flipped the equation of the relationship between humans and the spiritual realm and became God's servant, instead of a conniver and beggar. His interpretation -- that we are meant to seek God's guidance and obey it -- sent shock waves into the nations in whose territory he sojourned. Abraham also was a teacher. The Bible reports that he shared the spiritual treasure he had discovered and taught God's ways to his whole household, which included several hundred slaves. His words spread like rain on parched ground, a powerful teaching that filtered through the years, changing the people that it touched.

The descendants of Abraham (called Hebrews) embraced his concept of a Single God and an unchanging cannon of Law that protects all people equally. The laws of the Hebrews' God protected the rights of women, children, the poor, slaves, foreigners and those who caused accidental death. The punishments it required for theft were lenient, by comparison with their neighbors. Their economic rules were fair and socially stabilizing. Male slaves who accepted circumcision were set free after seven years. These were powerful incentives that drew many from other societies to be curious about the Invisible God that Abraham had identified. The weak and needy were drawn into the faith because of its fairness and protection. There they became strong and contributed to the community.

Jesus (4 B.C. – 29 A.D.) created a seismic shift in the way the Hebrew religion was practiced during his time. He threw out the additions and law denying interpretations rabbis had added to the Bible and completed the understanding of the Torah Law (given in the first five books of the Bible) by teaching its intentions. He replaced blood sacrifices with the self-sacrifice of fairness and service, sacrifices for sin with water baptism, stoning with scorning – a social "time out" for unrepentant rebels -- and tribal prejudice with outreach to all people. He taught and healed Samaritans and Gentiles to show that God loves all souls on Earth, and replaced the expectation of material blessings by teaching the rules for obedience to God and humility and the expectation of spiritual blessings. He taught forgiveness, which had been cut out of the Torah, and made men who were not even Levites into preachers and missionaries. He raised the status of women by speaking with them, healing them and teaching them, another sharp break with Hebrew tradition.

Muhammad (570-632 A.D.) who grew up in a sea of idol worshippers, grasped the importance of the teachings of Abraham, Moses and Jesus that we are meant to submit to guidance given by the Living Power that designed and created this world. He confounded his contemporaries, then converted many of them to his views, and dictated a book of spiritual poetry so exquisite it has shaped a religion practiced around the world and kept the Arabic language alive for over a thousand years.

The code of conduct that we find in the Bible, the principles for living that Jesus taught and the beautiful, moralistic poetry of the Qur'an all contain Abraham's teachings of a fixed set of laws, equality among people, fair rules for economics and social interaction and daily submission to the guidance of the One Eternally Living Spirit Who is All-Knowing, All-Powerful, Just and Compassionate.

Just as there are especially talented scientists who discover and articulate the laws that govern material nature, there have been a few who were especially sensitive to spiritual order who discovered and articulated laws of spiritual nature. These five – the Buddha, Confucius, Abraham, Jesus and Mohammed – each created a core of devotees who lived and taught their religious insights. Their disciples later wrote down the words of their champions in each faith, and rose up to spread their teachings.

These courageous movers and shakers had a vision of how people could create order and balance in their personal lives if they would apply certain laws of spiritual nature to their thoughts, words and actions. They dedicated their lives to convincing their contemporaries to listen to what they had to say, and to experiment with the disciplines they taught. Because men and women experienced spiritual awakening when they lived by those teachings, civilizations around the Earth were reshaped to come closer to conforming to the laws that govern spiritual nature. This has enabled people to live in larger groups and enjoy the benefits they offer.

LAWS OF SPIRITUAL NATURE

If you step off a cliff you will be held accountable to a law of physics, whether you know the law or not. Likewise, we are accountable to the laws that govern the spiritual realm, whether we know them or not. We enjoy life more and live more productively if we learn the laws of both realms and make our choices within their limits.

The Bible says that God's laws are innate in us, meaning that the laws of spiritual nature that are intended to bring order, peace and functionality to our lives are already known by our spirits. (DT 30:11-14) If we have suppressed this knowledge, we can nevertheless re-sensitize ourselves to recognize it again. It is up to us to seek to understand the laws that govern the material realm in order to be safe and comfortable here. Likewise, it is our responsibility to seek to understand the laws that govern spiritual nature in order to live peacefully and productively here, as well as to be prepared when we continue in the spiritual realm after we die here.

Just as conscientious parents try to guide their children to learn good behavior and life skills because they know what comes next – that is, that their children will grow up and have to make their own way in the adult world – out of love for us the Living Creator of the spiritual and material realms has communicated through those who sensitized themselves spiritually to guide us to learn the behavior and skills we need for what comes next – because we will all eventually die in the material realm and the soul we develop here will determine where we spend our time when we are in the spiritual realm. Our parents love us and when we make mistakes they try to comfort us, but certain laws and rules in nature and society can't be ignored and we break them to our peril. God also loves us, but the laws of spiritual nature are fixed. For us to be happy here, as well as in the spiritual realm, we must use our time here to learn and live these rules so we are prepared for today, and for what comes next.

Some things never change, they are just rediscovered and explained in the current vernacular. The Fundamental Laws that govern the spiritual realm never change but we need to be re-sensitized to their subtle power in each generation. In addition, many laws of spiritual nature, while they are used all over the world, are not deliberately studied or consciously applied. Using these laws in experiments helps us develop spiritual sensitivity so we may more easily apply these laws to our lives.

To that end, I've suggested some experiments to help develop spiritual sensitivity so that we may understand the value of applying these laws to ourselves and, ultimately, so we may more clearly perceive the daily guidance always available to us from the Living Designer and Creator of both spiritual and material nature. In this book I offer an introduction to twenty laws, as well as easy experiments that can be used to develop spiritual sensitivity and verify the laws.

As the most prominent religions have developed over the centuries, each has divided into various sects. Where quotes are available from the one who started the religion, I use those quotes to show how their originators all grasped and taught the same concepts that make up these laws of spiritual nature.

I refer to the original teachings of those who started each religion, though none of them wrote down their teachings. Even Muhammad, who was illiterate, dictated the Qur'an – of which we have no original manuscript. For the most part, their disciples were so awed by their teachers that they faithfully recorded some of their sayings. While over the generations uncomfortable and challenging principles and rules have been repressed, nevertheless their intent may be teased out from the original teachings that are available in the quotes attributed to the Masters. I also reference where these concepts are found in the *Egyptian Book of the Dead* and in what is written in current Hindu teachings.

As a quick reference, I have included charts of the five categories and twenty laws of spiritual nature that are covered in this book and a quote from each source as it speaks to these laws. I also have included definitions of the categories and laws, which you will find in three pages just before the charts.

Confucius told us to listen closely and choose what is best to live by. He said to watch closely what transpires, and keep a record of it. It is useful to keep a record of spiritual experiments. Just as scientists keep detailed notes of experiments so they can better evaluate the results, students of the laws of spiritual nature should keep a journal of experiments and review it from time to time to look for patterns and lessons. As with scientific societies, it also helps to compare notes about the results of spiritual experiments with other students of the laws that govern spiritual nature.

You wouldn't do a science experiment half way and expect to get the correct results. You should conduct spiritual experiments with the same attention to detail and lack of bias. If you try and don't get the expected result, re-check the instructions and your actions. Make corrections, and try again.

As you use the exercises in this book to experiment with some of the laws that govern spiritual nature, your spiritual sensitivity will be sharpened and the value of the laws will become clearer. What you may find in using the experiments and keeping a journal is that there appears to be an invisible string connecting thoughts, words and actions to events beyond your scope of seeing or controlling. Try to discern God's ultimately loving purpose in the responses that come as a result of experimenting with these laws.

CHAPTER TWO

ACCOUNTABILITY

Earth ticks like a well-made clock, made to balance while it adjusts. It works because it is balanced. It changes steadily and within strict limits. We who have free will constantly, even if subconsciously, seek balance to create good physical health, mental health and spiritual health, so we can work smoothly and productively as well.

Mechanics is a category of laws that helps engineers create material objects – from clocks to space craft -- that balance and function efficiently. Accountability is its equivalent in spiritual law. Accountability is our innate desire to achieve balance so we can function. We hold others accountable for their words and acts in our relationships, and we hold ourselves accountable and evaluate the consequences – whether helpful or not so much – of our own thoughts, words and acts according to what we have been taught and what we have learned through experience. Like applying the rules of mechanics helps engineers create objects that work dependably, applying the laws of accountability helps us achieve balance and sufficient harmony to create a network of relationships that functions in useful ways.

Our innate desire for balance is expressed in our desire for justice and forgiveness, give and take, work and rest and freedom and loyalty. When we act – or interact with others who act – against the laws that regulate these actions, it throws us out of balance.

Why do we need to constantly adjust and balance? It is because we are both material and spiritual beings. Like the Living Spirit that designed and created the universe, we have free will. Therefore, we must choose to conform ourselves to the laws that govern the material and spiritual realms since we are not created to do so by following instincts in all that we do. Because we are spiritual beings who live in the material realm, distractions, desires and fears can pressure us to act against the laws that govern our spiritual nature. Nevertheless, when we think, say or do something that disrupts our spiritual balance, we are able to reflect on the consequences we have caused and seek ways to create a better balance in ourselves and our relationships.

From ancient times priests have taught repentance. Of what could we or should we repent if we do not have free will, along with the sensitivity to recognize that some behaviors achieve better results than others and that we have the ability to change our behavior? Without free will there is no accountability. We have the power -- and therefore the responsibility -- to choose good behavior over bad behavior. When we make poor choices, we repent – we apologize and change our behavior in order to bring ourselves and our relationships into better balance. Likewise, when we look ahead and see that decisions we have made are taking us in a direction that could hurt us, we can imagine the likely result and change course.

The Great Designer-Creator Spirit does not force us against our will. We are not puppets of God. With every breath we take we have the freedom to exercise choice. Nevertheless, God created fixed laws to govern both material nature and spiritual nature. These laws create a natural, invisible force, or fence, within which we can make countless choices, but within which there are definite limits. When we break a law in either realm, we experience the repercussions.

In the Bible it is sometimes written that God has hardened someone's heart. When we choose against the laws that govern spiritual nature, we weaken our spiritual sensitivity. This throws us out of balance and may manifest as an unreasonable or selfish attitude – a hard heart. This is a natural effect caused by law breaking. God doesn't control our free will. However, God made the fixed law and when we break the law it destabilizes us and results in certain types of actions. Some have interpreted this as God "causing" the actions. Our free will, however, is still intact.

When someone usurps or manipulates another person's free will – such as in kidnapping, in slavery, in subliminal messaging (also called "priming") in ways that can happen in the military or by giving false information for the other to act on – they are interfering with the behavior for which the person is held accountable by spiritual law and it simultaneously impacts their own spiritual balance in this lifetime and, in the event they **reincarnate**, in another life as well. We are responsible for giving good example and advice and for not deliberately causing another person to go out of balance.

Muhammad warned that those who mislead others set themselves up for punishment. (S. 39:8) Giving misleading advice to children that could cause them to make spiritually damaging choices is a double tragedy. Jesus said that those who mislead children would be better off drowned with a millstone around their neck. (MT 18:5-10) This is because the imbalance they cause in their own spirits will eventually need to be corrected. They will be held accountable.

The **Golden Rule** – to treat others as you want to be treated yourself – means that our attitude, words and acts bounce back on ourselves. Confucius said that our humanity is shaped through interactions with others. There are no monks in Confucianism. Our words and actions exert a power that spreads like a ripple in a pond and changes our internal, as well as our social, environments to shape ourselves and our communities. The Golden Rule holds us accountable for choosing words and actions that have a positive impact on ourselves and our social environment.

An early recorded reference to accountability after death comes from the ancient *Egyptian Book of the Dead,* where we are told that the deceased's heart is weighed on a scale against forty-two moral rules. If it is weighed down by misconduct – even a feather's weight – the individual's after-life is condemned to an early and unpleasant end.

Hinduism, Buddhism, the Bible and the Qur'an all teach that there is something of us that is alive after our body dies, that it is judged, or evaluated, and that the judgment has an impact on our future. (Isaiah 26:19; MT 6:19-21, 10:28; LK 6:22-23) Psalm 15 (1-5) in the Bible asks, Who shall live with God? and answers: the upright. Jesus told us to lay up treasure in heaven – because we will live there. Muhammad said that anyone, male or female, who has faith in God and lives righteously will enter heaven. (S. 4:124) He also warned that the evil will live in hell fire. (S. 11:105-106) We are held accountable.

The prophet Daniel, the author of Revelation and Muhammad all taught that our deeds are recorded in a Book from which we are automatically evaluated when we die and our soul transitions into the spiritual realm. (Daniel 7:9-10, 10:22; Revelation 20:11-12) Muhammad said the Book will be open and all will be judged from what is in the Book. (S. 39:67-70, 18:47-49, 36:12)

Thoughts are things and they send out a (possibly electric) signal. The Bible says that God sees our thoughts. (Jeremiah 17:10; MT 6:5-8) Muhammad concurred. God reads our hearts and knows every way we are deceptive, he said. (S. 40:19, 2:284) What we think impacts our actions, so both are under the laws of spiritual nature.

Some who have had a Near Death Experience -- where they died and were revived -- report that they talked with departed loved ones on the other side of life and were told by them that they wished they had used their time on Earth to better develop their spirit. From their position on the other side of life they could see what a precious opportunity we have while we are in materiality to prepare ourselves for life in the spiritual realm. What we think, say and do while we are here determines the quality of the experience our spirit has after this life is over. What is material will pass away, but what is spiritual lives on past material death. To prepare for what comes next after material life, we should be diligent about firming up our flabby spirits while we have the opportunity in this life. Jesus, too, warned that what is bound on Earth is bound in Heaven. (MT 18:18)

One man who was revived after a Near Death Experience said he perceived that after death people gravitate into groups according to their soul's vibrations, which they created by the thoughts, words and acts they chose while they were on Earth. We need to be zealous in seeking spiritual knowledge and developing spiritual sensitivity and balance while we are here because that will help us make better decisions so we are better prepared for the inevitable accounting that comes when our spirits are released from the material realm.

Endurance is a weight that helps us stay in balance. Suicide is possible, but the spiritual consequences are extremely harsh. Several sources report that those who throw the gift of life away, whether deliberately or through carelessness, are placed in spiritual solitary confinement with no light or sound for the length of time they would normally have been alive on Earth. We are in this realm for the purpose of learning and developing spiritually. We must respect this unique opportunity and endure through pain, boredom, harsh conditions, injustice, fear, depression and desperation to drain every drop of spiritual learning from the cup before we leave.

Even if we live by ourselves, we have to endure the caprices of physical and environmental nature. When we live with just one other person, we also have to endure a range of personality differences and learn to be resilient with constant change. Living in a group requires us to expand our endurance skill set as our group lurches along, facing challenges and experimenting with various styles of response.

29

Pain and sorrow result from breaking (or being impacted by someone who is breaking) the fixed laws of material or spiritual nature. So, **self-discipline** – holding ourselves accountable -- and civil discipline – being held accountable by our governing body -- help us keep our balance as we maneuver the many layered social environment. When our self-discipline is poorly informed or weak and we create danger or social problems for ourselves or others, it helps us if our family, friends or community restrain us from continuing on a destructive trajectory, and guide us to make choices for better spiritual growth and material safety and success.

REINCARNATION

To the ancients, reincarnation was obvious. Just as plants die in the autumn and regenerate every spring, it was obvious that after humans die, they return as newborn babes.

Historically, the concept of reincarnation was taught very early in the religions of India. It was taught that words and acts create a record impressed on the spirit, and that this record carries over from one life to the next. Since our goal is to develop perfect spiritual balance, and we can't develop it in one lifetime, reincarnation gives us the opportunity to build it piece by piece. In the caste system, which is unique to Hinduism, it is maintained that souls are born into a fixed social status.

Other groups also have taught reincarnation. Gold tablets found in the graves of polytheists in Greece and Italy dating from the fifth century B.C. to the second century A.D. give instructions for how to guide the souls of the dead so they can avoid repeating in their coming life the errors they made in the past.

The Abrahamic religions of Judaism, Christianity and Islam have taught reincarnation. In Deuteronomy (30:4-5 TNJB) it is reported that God brings us back to Earth from the corners of Heaven. Psalm 90 (3-5) tells us that God brings us to dust, and in the morning we grow like grass. The likely reason why the Bible's writers didn't question why God told Rebekah the adult fate of the twins still in her womb is because they accepted that we all return to continue patterns we began in previous lives. (GN 25:21-26)

Zechariah (chapter 3) believed that the Messiah would be Joshua (Moses' helper) reincarnated. Malachi (3:23-24 (or at 4:5-6)) predicted that Elijah would reincarnate before the "Day of the Lord." In Luke (1:11-17) we are told that a baby (who later became known as John the Baptist) would be born with the spirit and power of Elijah. Jesus led his disciples to understand that John the Baptist was Elijah reincarnated. (MT 11:7-10, 17:10-13) John the Baptist said that Jesus had lived before him. Joshua lived before Elijah. (JN 1:15, 30)

When Jesus' disciple Peter asked about rewards for the apostles, Jesus said they would be richly rewarded in the "regeneration." (MT 19:27-29 G-E) The book of John reports that Jesus said that those who have done good will resurrect to a good life and those who have done evil will resurrect to judgment. (JN 5:28-29) In the Bible the same word that is now translated as resurrection (anastasis – literally the arising or coming back to life of the dead) can also be understood to mean reincarnation.

Jesus' parable about laborers hired at different times of the day but all paid the same was about reincarnation. Some souls labor here longer than others, but the ultimate reward -- eternal life with the Creator beyond time and substance -- is the same for all. (MT 20:1-16)

Paul, a prominent first century Christian teacher, expressed belief in reincarnation when he was on trial. (Acts 23:6,

24:14-16) As a result, we have a record that early Christians taught reincarnation. Records also show that it was part of the doctrine of the early Christian writers St. Clement of Alexandria (150-220) and of Origen (185-254) one of his students. The teaching of reincarnation did not come into disfavor until the church came under the influence of Emperor Constantine in the 4th century.

Muhammad also taught reincarnation. He said that some ask, who will cause them to come back to life? The One Who created you the first time, he answered. (S. 17:51) Consider how Allah gives life to the Earth after its death. Similarly, He gives life to those who are dead, for He has complete power. (S. 30:50) He causes the living to come from the dead, and the dead from the living. (S. 6:95)

In Jesus' day there was a raging debate between the Sadducees (the rich businessmen of his day) who denied reincarnation and the existence of the spiritual realm, and the law-conscious Pharisees, who taught the reality of both. Jesus taught both that we are alive after death and that we are judged in the spiritual realm. His gruesome death by crucifixion, followed by his resurrection, settled the debate. That he could appear and disappear at will, eat food, be touched and yet ascend into heaven in the sight of his followers proved the reality of the spiritual realm and that our spirits live there after our bodies die on Earth. (JN 20:1-29; LK 24:13-35; 1 Corinthians 15:3-7; Acts 1:1-11, 2:22-36) This also validated Jesus' teachings about how to live while we are on Earth in order to best prepare for our rebirth in the spiritual realm.

Revelation (3:10-13) affirms that those who live by God's Law become like pillars and "go out no more." After knowledge of the laws God created becomes a permanent, intimate part of us, we become able to perceive and choose God's daily guidance over our own willfulness and, therefore, we are able to sin no more -- because all sin is choosing our will over God's will. When we learn how to choose to

32

completely submit to God we are ready to blend back into our Creator's rhythm and return to God's place beyond time and substance for eternity. Then we go out/reincarnate no more.

Though Confucius did not address the issue of reincarnation, in Confucianism the tradition of ancestor worship is an acknowledgement that he believed that the spirit lives after the body dies.

Currently, Buddhists teach that we have a goal -- which they call Nirvana – and it is the end of reincarnation. In Hinduism it is said that the goal of life is to reach the Divine Essence by righteous living, and that this is liberation from the cycle of reincarnation.

The concept of reincarnation was made popular in America in the 1930's by Edgar Cayce, the "sleeping prophet." Mr. Cayce put himself into a self-induced trance and sought medical advice for people who consulted him. During this process he discovered that his clients had had previous lives which sometimes had an impact on their current health.

Since then several books have been written by those who have researched this subject. *Where Reincarnation and Biology Intersect,* one of the books by Ian Stevenson, M.D., and *Other Lives, Other Selves: A Jungian Psychotherapist Discovers Past Lives,* by Roger J. Woolger, Ph.D. are among those that examine reincarnation.

It is important to learn the laws that govern the spiritual realm, because doing so can help us disentangle from severe repercussions that could come to us as a result of having broken laws in the past. Learning the fixed laws of spiritual nature and choosing to live by them has the power to rehabilitate our damaged spirit and strengthen us as we inevitably meet again tests that made us stumble in the past, whether in this life or previous lives.

Even though you expect someone who is important to you to reincarnate, sometimes when someone you feel deeply about dies it may bring up a wave of emotions that makes it difficult to function as you normally would. At those times it may be useful to write a letter to the deceased and pour out your feelings – what you wish you had said to him or her when they were alive. Then find a quiet place for an uninterrupted period of time and read the letter out loud to the person's spirit – because their spirit will still be present with you. It can help the process of healing to begin when you articulate your feelings and share them with the one who you feel deeply about. That person's living spirit is waiting to hear your thoughts.

This is useful as a one time experience to enable you to put some emotions to rest and regain function in your life. Be careful you do not cross the line and ask for guidance from the spirit of the dead. The Spirit of God is each soul's personal guide. God has all knowledge and desires to lead us spiritually.

Perhaps because our spirit continues to live after our body dies, is why there are traditions to show respect to the deceased shortly after death. Instructions given in the Bible say that if you have been in the presence of a dead body you should not engage in social activities or eat meat for seven days, and you should be sprinkled with water for purification on the third and seventh days. (NU 19:11-12, 14-19) Water for purification, it says, is made by burning to ashes meat from an unworked red heifer, cedar wood, deep red material and hyssop. The sprinkling would be done as the day begins (in the evening before) on the third and seventh days. This may be a way to show acknowledgement and respect to the deceased.

Because the corrections we experience when we reincarnate into the material realm are natural and useful is not an excuse to refuse to give emergency aid where it is needed. For example, the Bible warns that anyone who misleads someone who is blind will draw a curse onto himself. (DT 27:18) Confucius taught that special consideration should be given to the blind. We should explain where to walk and sit, and inform them of who is present. (A. 15.41) When Jesus healed the man born blind, he said that he had not sinned previously but that he was born blind so that the works of God would be shown in him. His healing brought many to pay attention to Jesus' teachings. Also, helping the needy is an expression of the Golden Rule and it helps our own souls grow in love and humility, spiritual attributes we all need to develop.

It isn't for us to condemn other souls. There isn't any sin a human can commit that we all couldn't be tempted to commit given the same chemistry and circumstances. God loves all souls, and we must love all souls and give compassionate aid where it is needed.

Corrections according to the fixed laws of spiritual nature are inevitable and useful. It is not necessary for us to increase a punishment with a rejecting attitude or by refusing to help those in need. In the Bible we are told to give emergency help even to enemies. It builds good qualities in our own spirit and in our family and community soul groups when we work to relieve the suffering of others.

In addition, new cycles of injustice and imbalance are created constantly. Anyone can get caught up in a new cycle even if they didn't create it. Jeremiah and his scribe Baruch tried repeatedly to warn the political leaders of their day of their impending doom. The leaders ignored the warnings. When tragedy finally came, Baruch complained that God had added grief to his pain. God's message to Baruch, through the prophet Jeremiah, was: "Behold, that which I have built, I will break down, and that which I have planted I will pluck up in this whole land, and you want great things for yourself? Seek them not, for I am bringing evil on all flesh." (Jeremiah 45:3-5)

Those who are caught up in a tragedy may not have caused it. When we become aware of injustice or tragedy, we should do what we can to relieve it. Those who knowingly cause injustice or disaster will eventually lead themselves into correcting experiences. We would become infected with their rhythm of rebellion if we responded to them with excessive revenge and by not bringing them to a court of law where their defense can be heard.

In each life, we explore life's many facets – its joys and sorrows, its mysteries and revelations. We meet again foes and friends we knew before and receive back advice and actions we gave previously. Eventually, each soul will tire of the cycles and seek the way out.

While it is the ultimate goal of each soul to have a "last life" here, our addiction to the distractions and demands of materiality is hard to break. Some of us anesthetize ourselves with comfort theology slogans, such as, "Jesus did it all for me," or that everyone who is born of the lineage of Abraham is saved by that genetic relationship, no matter how they behave.

Did God capriciously choose Abraham, or did God choose Abraham because Abraham chose to seek and respond to the "Creator of Heaven and Earth"? According to the Bible, God said that **if** they chose His will **then** the Hebrews would be for Him a nation of priests -- indicating that free will choice is necessary. In addition, by the rule that every circumcised male who chooses to follow God's rules is equal to the Hebrews, it is obvious that those "chosen" are all those who choose God. (EX 12:48, 19:3-6)

With comfort theology slogans we pretend that Heaven is a free gift for all who repeat the slogan, no matter how execrable they may be in their behavior. We'd like to be accepted back into God's presence without giving up our carelessness, arrogance or rebellion, and so we claim that all will go to Heaven who come under the magic wand of the slogan. But neither Moses nor Jesus ever claimed that. In fact, they taught just the opposite. They taught accountability.

Moses taught accountability to the laws written in the Bible, and predicted that those who don't live by them will draw punishments onto themselves. (LV 26:14-43) We must rebalance our spiritual energies so they are compatible with that of the Great Spirit that designed and created both realms. Then we may naturally transition back into God's place when our sojourn here comes to its end.

Jesus said that those who do God's will and those who oppose God are separated like wheat and thorns, sheep and goats and good fish and bad fish when their spirits transition into the spiritual realm. (MT 13:47-50) We are evaluated after we die, and we are held accountable according to the laws that govern the spiritual realm. There is no magic wand that lets us return to God's Place without our deliberate preparation to do so.

Reincarnation is good news if you are holding yourself accountable and trying to develop spiritual sensitivity so you may perceive and submit to God's daily guidance and return to being one will with your Creator. The teaching of reincarnation is a timely warning if you are creating problems that will have repercussions you don't want to come back to experience.

REINCARNATION EXPERIMENT

Write down one of your current circumstances that strongly affects you. Meditate and ask God to reveal to you how decisions and acts in previous lives may be having an impact on your current circumstances.

A simple meditation technique is to lie down wearing loose clothing and no shoes. Clear your mind of judgments and fears, and open up your curiosity. Breathe in and out slowly and deeply five times – drawing oxygen through your toes to the top of your head each time.

Let go of your preconceptions. Ask God to reveal to you how you interacted in previous times with someone who is involved in the circumstance that concerns you. Let God and your own spirit guide your perceptions. Perhaps you will start with a family member, and during subsequent sessions expand to friends, work associates, neighbors and others. Be honest and courageous. If you practice this as a regular discipline, over time you will build sensitivity and perceptions and find a variety of ways to understand and interact with the people around you.

When you are finished with your meditation exercise, take five deep breaths centered in your chest before you get up.

THE GOLDEN RULE

If everyone lived by the Golden Rule – to treat all others as they want to be treated – there would be no murder or war, because no one wants to be killed or attacked. There would be no economic injustice, because no one wants to be personally or nationally impoverished by another.

To treat others as we want them to treat us is an eternal law of spiritual nature. No civilization can be sustained without the majority of its citizens living by this law. When we don't treat others as we want to be treated, society dissolves into distrust, hate and revenge. This fixed law of spiritual nature is always true. When we live by it we develop better balance within ourselves and in our society and world.

The Golden Rule is an integral part of the teaching of karma, the principle of inevitable consequences, held by both Hindus and Buddhists.

Confucius was well aware of this spiritual law. When asked if there is a single word by which one could guide one's life he replied, "reciprocity" -- don't do to others what you don't want done to you. (A. 15.23) This rule is forever. Articulating this law is the genius of a few spiritual masters.

Jesus drew the Golden Rule from the Hebrew text of Leviticus 19:34. (MT 7:12) He said that the first (the most important) law is that God is One and we are to love God with all our heart, soul, mind and strength. Then he said that to love our neighbors as ourselves is like it, elevating the Golden Rule to be of equal status with the First Law. Teaching his followers to live by the Golden Rule was the basis of Jesus' prediction that the world will know his followers by their love. (JN 13:34-35; MT 22:36-40)

The Golden Rule is not as prominent in Jewish teachings as it is in Christian teachings. A Jewish man once told me that if he was born Muslim or Christian he would want to be punished with unfair treatment. He missed the meaning of this rule. He should have asked himself whether he wanted others to be prejudiced against him because of his religious affiliation. If not, then neither should he be prejudiced and unfair to others because of their religious affiliation. According to the impartial laws that govern our spirits, anyone who treats another person with prejudice should expect like treatment in return.

Nevertheless, one of the reasons the Hebrew's system of laws became popular and caused changes in other law codes is because its laws require kindness and fairness. Beyond just maintaining social order, as did the rules of many of the polytheistic religions, the Bible's laws require generosity and protection for the weak. The gleaning law -- the law to allow the poor and travelers to eat produce left in the field -- the laws to help widows, orphans and foreigners, the cancellation of debts and release of slaves every seven (and every 50th) years, the privileges of citizenship after male circumcision and assuring foreigners equal protection under the law were all major legal advancements for their day that have helped to shape civilizations. (DT 24:17-22, 14:28-29, 23:24-25, 15:7-15; LV 19:9-10, 24:22; EX 23:9)

The Golden Rule is reflected in Islam where it is said that those who cause good for others are drawn into good events; those who cause evil for others are drawn into evil events. (S. 4:85)

Closer to our own day, philosopher Immanuel Kant (1724-1804) who wrote extensively on religion, morals and philosophy, struggled with this concept and finally re-wrote it as: "Act only according to that maxim whereby you can at the same time will that it should become a universal law." (*Groundwork of the Metaphysics of Morals,* by Immanuel Kant, 1785) Even those who doubt God's existence recognize this as a fixed law necessary for personal and social balance.

Of course, not everyone would want to be treated exactly as you might like to treat yourself. Besides different ages and genders there are different cultures and circumstances. To practice the Golden Rule, we need to have well developed listening and communicating skills in order to find out what other people need and want, their beliefs and goals and how they interpret our words and actions.

The aim is the same, because all people want to be treated with honesty, respect and consideration. But the actual details will vary. As we strain to understand one another and learn how to accommodate each other we build spiritual sensitivity.

Looking around the world we see that the Golden Rule, in some form, is part of every nation's cultural heritage. Too often, however, it is overlooked or applied selectively. It should be taught through stories, games and songs throughout the school years, so that citizens everywhere become more sensitive about how their behavior affects others. This would lead us to develop a sustainable economic model worldwide, and to have more sustainable environmental practices as well as more peaceful relations between people at every scale.

GOLDEN RULE EXPERIMENT

With friends, keep in mind that you will want to have friends to share special times and information with as life goes on. So, when you disagree with your friends, always consider how you would like to be treated, and speak and act towards them as if you are speaking and acting towards yourself. Learn how to listen to your friends and ask questions for clarity and understanding.

If you have children, think how you would like to be treated if you reincarnate into another life and one of your children in this life becomes one of your parents in the next. Treat your children the way you would like to be treated should you return as one of their children. Practice listening to each child's concerns and interpretations of events and desires.

With spouses, employing the Golden Rule requires an extra level of sensitivity because men and women, being chromosomally and hormonally different, interpret life differently and have different emotions and desires. Some needs are the same, such as the needs for respect, communication, appreciation, support and cooperation. But there are many levels of understanding and experience within each person's needs. It is important to ask questions and listen to your spouse to find out how you can please him or her – because you want to be pleased, even if in a different way. Recognizing that you interpret some things differently, talk about how to work compatibly for shared goals and how to support one another's unique needs.

Listening well to what others say is a required skill in order to exercise the Golden Rule effectively. So, you might research games that teach listening skills to use with your family and at some social gatherings. One such game is,

"What Do You See?" Everyone in a group says in turn what they see – how they interpret or what does it remind them of – a single verse, section of scripture, event or social issue. You could inform participants several days in advance so they have time to reflect on the topic. Each participant has one minute at the beginning to summarize what they heard the previous speaker say, and then three minutes to give their own opinion uninterrupted. Go around more than once so responses can be made to other speakers. A large clock that has a second hand helps keep everyone on time.

ENDURANCE

Endurance is the art and science of Buddhism. The Buddha saw life as full of suffering, and suffering as something we can overcome through right living, deep meditation exercises and withdrawal from activities. He advised monks to mentally move beyond their physical needs and desires and to train themselves to endure all environmental conditions, as well as sickness, hunger and thirst. The goal is to be as free as possible from all attachments to life while yet remaining alive.

Confucius taught that we develop our humanity through interaction with others. Interactions often require patience and endurance. A noble person stays steadfast throughout suffering, he said. (A 15.2)

According to the Abrahamic faiths, enduring the trials of this life, and seeking God's guidance to change what we can, helps develop spiritual sensitivity as we experience God's presence and learn to trust God's guidance. We should ask God in "listening prayer" what we should learn from a stressful or unjust experience, and how to endure or change it.

Jesus didn't complain. He was often without shelter and food. He was expelled from synagogues and towns. He was attacked verbally and with stones. He was betrayed by a friend, falsely accused, tortured and executed. Through it all he did not curse or deny God. As he was dying, he asked God to forgive those who tormented him. We are all here because we chose our will over God's will, so the unpleasant things that happen to us here should spur us to diligently seek what we need to do to choose God's will first in our lives and return to the beauty, safety and peace of God's place.

That suffering is good for the soul is an ancient concept. Jesus taught us how to endure deep injustice and torture and thereby overcome all ties to this world through trust and obedience to God. Don't fear those who kill the body; fear the One who can destroy both body and soul in hell, he said. (MT 10:28) We must keep choosing the fixed spiritual law over succumbing to the lures and threats that are a natural part of the material realm. Jesus said that those who endure to the end will be saved. (MK 13:13)

Jesus was tested, and he predicted that his followers would be tested, too. (MT 10:17-31; LK 22:28) He told us to expect tribulation in this world and to anticipate that those who hate him will hate his followers as well. (JN 15:18-21) He predicted that family and friends would betray one another, and that when someone murders a follower of Christ he will think he is doing a good thing. (LK 21:12-18; JN 16:1-2) Nevertheless, he said, we should be brave in the face of these challenges, and endure. (MT 16:24-27)

Muhammad concurred. Do you think you'll go to Heaven without being tested? he asked. (S. 2:214) Allah tests us with trauma, unmet needs and loss, but those who patiently persevere will rejoice. (S. 2:155, 3:186, 200, 8:46)

When life is unpleasant we must endure it, learn from it, seek God through it and follow God's guidance to make a contribution to our family and community, and to relieve suffering if we can. Early Christians endured persecution – beheadings, crucifixions, being burned at the stake, thrown to wild beasts and other kinds of torture -- because they had experienced the truth of Jesus' words when they applied his teachings to their lives, and they believed his message.

While the religious are still persecuted with violence and injustice in many parts of the world today, in some countries some who are self-satisfied struggle to endure even their denomination's rituals, rules and traditions. They weakly allow themselves to be conformed to the world, instead of working to conform the world to God-seeking and spiritual sensitivity. Torture isn't necessary in order to practice endurance. We can take up a spiritual challenge and endure through the process.

According to many religions, humans chose to turn from God. In the Bible, the Garden of Eden story is a symbol of how we chose our will over God's will. Adam (mankind) and Eve (the beginning) fell by accepting the fruit (consequences) of the lie we all stumble over – that we can choose our will over our Maker's and not experience correction for it. Everything we experience – from irritating gnats to the horrors of war – is a consequence of that rebellion. Humble, even joyful, endurance is a necessary part of the spiritual equation that leads us to develop spiritual sensitivity and come into balance with the Great Spirit that designed and created both realms.

Learning patience helps us develop the spiritual muscle of endurance. Learning how to wait, and when and how to act, is a spiritual skill. Jesus told us to be as persistent in prayer as a suffering widow, and as persistent as a man who begs from his neighbor in the middle of the night. (LK 11:5-13, 18:1-8) Being patient while enduring, we learn to ardently seek God and God's guidance.

ENDURANCE EXPERIMENT

Patience is a stepping stone to endurance. If we learn patience, we may learn how to persevere until we understand more than we originally thought to ask. By learning patience, we learn how to endure at those times when we must.

Learning gardening skills takes patience. Planting fruit, herb or vegetable seeds in the ground, in containers, in a vertical garden or elsewhere requires us to be patient. Seeds take months to bear fruit, and many things can go wrong and spoil the crop. With gardening, we must reflect on what each type of seed needs in order to grow and bear fruit.

Different plants need different kinds of food. It is important to first learn what is the best soil food for the type of plants you grow. Also, some plants grow better when planted with companion plants. Some people say that rain water is better than tap (chlorinated) water for plants. There are those who believe that talking to their plants and playing music to them helps them grow. As you watch your plants grow, try to find out why some don't grow as they should or bear fruit.

To help us with gardening's learning curve, many universities offer a Master Gardening course that is open to part-time students and that includes gardening information for city dwellers. Backyard square foot gardens (at least 50 feet from a roadway, to avoid toxic auto exhaust) as well as vertical, hydroponic and container gardens are good for the environment and for healthy living.

If you don't want to take a college course, another source of gardening information is the Rodale series of books, which have been guiding gardeners for over 50 years.

Compost is an important component of gardening. Vegetative kitchen scraps (that have not been with eaten food) and garden waste such as leaves and cuttings become new dirt that nourishes plant life. Even apartment dwellers can compost kitchen scraps. Special containers that control odors are made for kitchen composting. The book, *Compost City,* by Rebecca Louie is a good resource for city dwellers.

Also, your state environmental office can tell you if there is a community composting program in your area. You can find composting and recycling charts on the Internet, along with a wealth of other useful environmental information.

Some public and private schools teach gardening skills. It is a wonderful life skill to enter adulthood knowing how to safely create compost and plant, manage, harvest and preserve food. It helps students develop respect for the rhythms of nature and encourages sustainable living in other ways as well. *Ecological Literacy, Education and the Transition to a Postmodern World*, by David W. Orr and *Ecological Literacy, Educating Our Children for a Sustainable World*, edited by Michael K. Stone and Zenobia Barlow give ideas for how to develop community support for teaching gardening in schools.

As we learn gardening skills we become more sensitive to the rhythms, cycles and needs of nature and we strengthen our ability to work with, instead of against, the environment. Simultaneously, we learn the skills to dig deep for information, see what is usable in what we might otherwise discard, and persevere when we might otherwise give up. We learn to endure.

SELF-DISCIPLINE

Astrophysicists tell us that it was about one second after the Big Bang that order – or law – was imposed on chaos. First there was matter -- in chaos. Then laws were imposed to cause systems to develop according to a specific design.

Spiritually, we must choose to impose some laws on ourselves. The laws may be known and written, and governments may hire people to enforce some of them, but beyond that we must choose self-discipline and live by the laws that govern us spiritually. Enter religion. One role of religion is to remind us by stories, songs and rituals about the Fundamental Laws of human conduct, and to exhort us to live by them. Receiving this message on a recurring basis, we become self-disciplined, which brings about a spiritual design that causes peace in ourselves and spreads out to our relationships.

Confucius said he was opposed to laws, but his definition of a noble person shows that he expected everyone to choose to behave according to fixed laws of spiritual nature. He was a master psychologist. He didn't insist that people follow his teachings. He simply defined nobility as virtue. Knowing that most of us like to think of ourselves as noble, he knew that this would draw us to act virtuously. He defined virtue as living without murder, theft, lying, sexual deviancy and covetousness. A noble person is concerned with what is just, he said, a vulgar man is concerned with what is expedient. (A. 4.16)

Confucius also said that to be fully human, one must impose control on one's self, and observe the rites. There are six rites: the celebration of birth, adulthood (called capping) marriage, anniversaries, death (mourning) and memorial services. Don't look at, say, listen to or do anything improper, he said. (A. 12.1) When angry, consider the consequences. If you gain an advantage, ask yourself if it is fair. (A. 16.10) Confucius taught self-discipline.

The Buddha defined self-discipline in detail in his Noble Eight Fold Path. The eight areas of self-discipline that he gave are: right views (reasoning) right intent (focus) right speech (honesty, no crude language and no pointless talk) right conduct (don't kill, steal, engage in unlawful sexual intercourse, covet or drink intoxicants) right livelihood (your occupation should be monastic, or at least promote life) right effort (endure all) right mindfulness (positive thinking, and to be free from lust, ill-will and cruelty) and right concentration (yoga for meditation). Self-discipline overcomes suffering, he would say.

After reminding the Hebrews to keep the laws he had been given on Mt. Sinai, Moses said, "I set before you life and death, blessing and curse. Choose life!" (DT 30:19) The law is known. It is up to us to be self-disciplined and choose it.

In the Bible, the prophet Isaiah (24:5-6) complained that the Earth had become defiled because people didn't keep God's Law. Jeremiah (5:1-9, 2:19-22) reported that the Hebrews had rebelled and had thrown off the yoke of God's Law. Moses wrote that if you know the Law and don't keep it, you show contempt for God's word and are to be separated from the community. (NU 15:30-31)

Centuries later, Jesus complained that rabbis had added to and changed to make ineffective some of the laws Moses had written for the Hebrews. He said they worshipped God in vain because they taught as if they were laws rules made up by themselves. (MT 15:7-9) This is another example of humans choosing our will over God's will. Jesus threw out the rabbinic additions and changes to the Bible and taught his followers to live by the intentions of the Biblical Law that had been written by Moses.

When a man asked him how to have eternal life, Jesus asked the man if he lived by the laws: don't kill, don't steal, don't bear false witness, don't commit adultery, honor your parents and love your neighbor as yourself. (MT. 19:16-19) The law is known. We are expected to live by it. He also said that those who keep and teach the Law will be considered great by those in the Kingdom of Heaven, and that those who don't keep the Law will be considered as less by those in the Kingdom of Heaven. (MT 5:19)

Though some interpret Paul as saying that Christians are justified by faith and don't have to live by the Law, Paul consistently taught his converts to live by God's rules. (See Romans 7:12; Galatians 5:16-23, 6:7-8 and Ephesians 5:3-6) "Do you not know that you are the temple of God and that the Spirit of God is living in you? Whoever defiles the temple of God, God will destroy: for the temple of God is holy, and that temple you are," he said. (1 Corinthians 3:16-17)

Muhammad said that Muslims believe in the revelations given through Abraham, Moses and Jesus. This would include the laws in the Bible. (S. 2:136 and 3:84, 3:3) In the Qur'an, Muhammad includes all the laws in the Ten Commandments except for the seventh day Sabbath. He also elaborates on many Biblical laws. (S. 6:151-155)

In Hinduism, the exercise of self-discipline is one of the Four Paths one may take to achieve liberation from reincarnation. Hindu teachers say that to begin any of the Four Paths we must first cleanse our spirit by not injuring any animal, by not lying, stealing, or lusting, and by overcoming greed. In addition, Hindus are taught physical and mental self-control through yoga and meditation.

In the same way that physical exercise strengthens the body, the religious the world over know that being self-disciplined is an exercise that sensitizes and strengthens us spiritually. Self-discipline makes success more likely in our careers and relationships, because it provides spiritual and mental stability, order, focus, functionality and vitality.

There is more than one level of meaning, even to the seven Fundamental Laws. Explaining a detail of the law to not kill, the Bible says to put a fence around your (flat) roof to prevent anyone from falling off, or you will be accountable for their injury. This means we should exercise self-discipline and plan ahead to avoid causing injury or illness to others. We are accountable if we cause physical harm to others. (GN 9:5; DT 22:8) This rule has broad implications for business owners and government decision makers! Businesses should not use processes that cause harm to the environment or that will cause harm to humans, because they will be held accountable spiritually, if not by civil laws.

There are other levels of meaning for this law. According to the Bible, pregnant women should receive special protection. It says that if men when fighting cause a pregnant woman to miscarry but no other damage results, the one who caused the unborn child's death should pay a fine set by her husband and approved by the judges. If the pregnant woman is injured, however, whoever caused the injury should have the very same injury done to him. If when fighting he caused the pregnant woman's death, he should be put to death. (EX 21:22-25)

Other Bible laws require compensation for personal injury. When people quarrel and attack one another and one of them is injured to such an extent that he must initially stay in bed though he is eventually able to walk, his assailant should pay for the time the injured man loses from employment and for his full cure. (EX 21:18-19) Anyone who permanently disfigures someone else should be disfigured in the same way. (LV 24:19-20)

Jesus' saying that, contrary to an eye for an eye, we should not resist evil, seems to negate the law at Leviticus 24:19-20. (MT 5:38-39) However, the Leviticus rule is only the reverse of the Golden Rule. Don't do to someone else what you don't want done to you. By designating an "evil person," Jesus may have meant an unjust person with power. In that event, it is safer to try to shame the bully by presenting the other cheek. In the case of disfigurement, we would expect the matter to be taken to a court of law.

Self-discipline also includes limiting our material possessions. Buddhism teaches that the way to avoid suffering is to not desire anything. Be content with whatever comes to you. There are ascetic sects in India's religions. Jesus said the deception of riches chokes the word of God. (MT 13:22) He taught us to overcome the world in ourselves and to make spiritual values our first priority – over family, over security and over personal desires. (MT 6:25-34; LK 14:26-27; JN 16:33) Muhammad reminded us that money isn't permanent. It is better to seek God's blessings. (S. 28:60)

The Bible tells us we are meant to "be holy" – in other words, to set ourselves apart (from excessive material indulgences) for God. (LV 20:7) The way Moses said it was to "circumcise your heart," in other words, limit our desires. (DT 10:16) The world is full of opportunities. To succeed spiritually we must stay focused and dedicated to our spiritual goal, carefully selecting from the wealth of opportunities available to us.

The correct interpretation of the law given in the Ten Commandments that we must not covet is: "don't set your heart on," meaning, don't scheme to take what belongs to someone else. (EX 20:17; DT 5:21) Muhammad warned against bribing judges to let you take another's land. (S. 2:188)   In the *Egyptian Book of the Dead*, the petitioner said he had not behaved deceitfully and had not stolen anyone's land. (16, 17) To not covet is a spiritual law that has been known since the beginning of recorded history.

The Bible and the Qur'an are full of financial advice designed to safeguard social stability. Both forbid exploiting the poor. (DT 24:14-15; LV 19:13; S. 30:38-39) Both forbid usury (i.e., interest, compound interest and stock and bond dividends). (DT 23:20-21; EX 22:25; LV 25:35-38; S. 2:275) Muhammad urged the rich to share with those who are in need. (S. 24:22) Likewise, the Bible tells us to cancel all debts every seven years for those who worship the One God. (DT 15:1-10) The Bible says to leave gleanings, the excess of our production, so the poor have that advantage. (LV 19:10; DT 24:20-22) Muslims are told that it is a sin to waste money, and that charity to the poor is pleasing to God and helps atone for sins. (S. 4:29, 92:4-10) In all these ways we set ourselves apart from excessive material indulgences and open ourselves up to spiritual sensitivity.

All of the religions that have shaped the longest lasting civilizations forbid sexual deviancy. There is no major religion that does not consider sexual deviancy to be against the laws of both material nature and spiritual nature. Over millennia humans have learned that rejection of and hatred for one gender over another gender – which is implicit in homosexual and lesbian relationships -- tears society apart and impedes its forward momentum. In addition, long before the Bible was written, some ancient societies had rules against rape and incest.

One of the justifications for the Hebrew's war against the inhabitants of Canaan was the Canaanites' sexual practices, which were immoral according to Biblical law. All types of sexual deviancy are social aberrations that are disruptive to individuals and to society because, among other things, they are a result of excessive selfishness that often leads to disloyalty. Deviancy also violates the trust within families because it feeds the desires of one gender by either exploiting or debasing the other.

The self-discipline required for spiritual seeking lifts society out of its animal nature and creates the process by which we develop mentally and emotionally. Only humans lift ourselves out of our animal nature by sometimes choosing to put aside the instinct to procreate and instead explore other goals. Exercising the powers of free will and self-discipline to do this has enabled us to shape ourselves and our world differently from that of other animals.

The Buddha taught monks to train to be free of sexual desires. He declared that he also had become free of sexual desire. One of the Five Moral Principles of Hinduism is control of sexual appetites. Confucius said a noble person should guard against lust, anger and forceful behavior. Lewd carousing leads to bad habits, as does extravagance and idleness, he said. (A. 16.7) Muhammad told Muslims to stay chaste until marriage, and he forbade incest. (S. 24:33, 4:22-23) Bible laws forbid rape and incest. (DT 22:23-29;

Leviticus 18; DT 27) Taking that a step further, the Bible tells us that the country vomits out its people when sexual self-discipline is not maintained. (LV 20:10-23) Because we are not wholly animal we damage ourselves spiritually if we pursue physical pleasure to the exclusion of the laws that govern the health and development of our spiritual nature.

"I didn't commit adultery," is one of the claims of a petitioner found in the ancient *Egyptian Book of the Dead*. (12) All three Abrahamic religions forbid adultery, prostitution and homosexuality. (EX 20:14; DT 5:18; LV 19:29, 21:9, 18:20; S. 7:81; GN 19:1-28 (oral sex)) In the Bible it is said that neither the earnings of a prostitute nor those of a dog (a homosexual) are to be given as an offering to God because both occupations are abhorrent to God. (DT 23:18) Likewise, Jesus, who quoted and referred to Deuteronomy more often than any other book, said to not give pearls (of wisdom) to pigs (prostitutes) or holy things to dogs (homosexuals). (MT 7:6) Muhammad said that homosexuals exceed all the bounds. (S. 26:165-166)

If you were to eat poison your family and friends would still love you -- and God would still love you -- but because you broke a law of material nature you would get very sick, and possibly die. When you break a law of spiritual nature you become spiritually sick even though God and your family and friends go on loving you. The laws are set. It is everyone's responsibility to learn and live by the laws of both material nature and spiritual nature. Self-discipline is one of those laws.

Self-discipline is a necessary part of having and enjoying our power and freedoms. Disciplining ourselves to live within the limits of the laws that govern us spiritually helps us create balance in ourselves and our relationships. Like all laws, self-discipline is imposed on chaos to create order.

SELF-DISCIPLINE EXPERIMENT

Throughout history people have fasted in order to clear their minds and bodies of distracting influences. Muhammad, as well as the Hebrews, fasted in order to develop self-discipline and spiritual sensitivity. (40 day fasts EX 24:18, 34:28; DT 9:9; MT 4:2; S. 2:183; LV 16:29-31) Muhammad also advised us to not use liquor, gambling or divination. (S. 5:90) The Muslim month long observance of Ramadan – when food is eaten only before sunrise and after sundown – is a fast meant to heighten spiritual sensitivity.

Our free will is powerfully impacted by our body chemistry. There is a direct link between the beverages and foods that we drink and eat and our emotions and thoughts, because their chemicals interact with our body's chemistry and impact our nervous system and brain. When we don't recognize the impact of diet on our emotions, we might even question if we have free will. As Paul said, "The good that I would I do not but the evil which I would not, that I do." (Romans 7:14-25) Even if we earnestly desire to live by moral principles, our best intentions can get caught up in conflicting emotional currents. There is a way to increase our self-control, but we need to first exercise self-discipline over our food choices.

It's possible to choose foods and beverages that increase our clarity of thought and self-control. But how difficult it is to exercise self-discipline over our taste buds and the social pressures that impact our food choices! On the other hand, if we can't control even our taste buds, then we compromise our free will – we relinquish a portion of it to taste sensations and their related chemicals.

The Bible gives clear rules about food. It tells us that fat and blood should never be eaten. In fact, fat and blood were once given in daily sacrifice at the temple in Jerusalem to underscore the importance of this law. Pork has fat within its meat that can't be cut out, so it is forbidden. Hamburger has some fat in it, so it shouldn't be eaten. (Leviticus 3:17) Shellfish are forbidden. Shellfish feed on waste and heavy chemicals and may carry elements that can cause disease in humans. Other categories of forbidden foods are birds and mammals that eat rodents, as well as all that move on their belly, such as snakes. (Leviticus 11) Muhammad also wrote about food rules. (S. 6:145) Salt is essential for cell function. In the Bible we are told that we must add salt to all grain foods. (Leviticus 2:13) It only takes a little bit of self-discipline to follow these simple food laws.

In addition, you may have noticed that the human diet didn't include artificial additives until very recently. In the 1970's, Ben Feingold, M.D. discovered that eliminating foods with artificial additives from the diet, as well as foods that contain the natural element salicylate, radically reduced pain, depression and nervous tension in his patients. It also increased their ability to focus and persevere in tasks. This diet is now used by many around the world as an alternative to drugs, which may have many dangerous side effects.

The Feingold Diet is simple. To begin with, read ingredients labels and don't eat any foods or drinks (or use chewing gum or cigarettes) that have artificial ingredients. To help you keep this diet you could select some recipes and make prepared foods such as energy bars and granola from scratch. It doesn't take very much time once you have collected the spices and ingredients for the foods you like.

There is a second tier to the diet, and that is to avoid plant foods that contain the natural chemical salicylate. This chemical is found in common foods such as chocolate, almonds, tomatoes, cucumbers, mints, grapes, berries, oranges, apples, plums, peaches, papaya, guava and oregano. It is also the element in aspirin. A full list is available from the Feingold Association.

So, what would you eat? Eat organic meats, fish and poultry, eggs and dairy products, nuts, lemons, limes, grapefruit, persimmons, pears, bananas, coconut, all melons, apricots, dates, figs, quince, autumn olives, paw paws, coffee, plain black tea (I would advise against green tea!) clover and buckwheat honey, sugar (I would avoid stevia) and all grain foods, legumes (i.e., beans, peas and lentils) and the many vegetables that do not contain salicylate. This is a great time to experiment with fruits and vegetables you haven't tried before, too. You may find some new favorites.

In addition, you should have either meat or eggs, or a diet that combines a carbohydrate, a dairy product and a legume at each meal. This is a high protein combination that gives you energy and stamina and is also good for your brain.

To increase your self-control over your free will, combine the Bible's food laws, the Feingold Diet and the meat/eggs or carbohydrate-legume-dairy diet in an experiment for seven weeks. The first 3 to 4 days will be the most difficult, as your body experiences withdrawal from foods to which you are accustomed. It gets easier after that.

Like any scientist, you should keep a journal, or log, of the effects of the diet. At the end of the seven weeks, review your journal and make a list of the ways the diet impacted your ability to exercise self-control more easily and live a calmer, more productive life.

CHAPTER THREE

COMMUNICATION

It isn't the size of our brains that gives us intelligence and rich, diverse, symbolic languages. Elephants have larger brains than ours. It is the desire for continual improvement of our circumstances which compels us to articulate what we learn outside of copying, and to teach what we know in detail to others.

As far as we know, all life forms communicate with their kind in some way – even plants. Primitive people believed that animals and plants also communicated with them. Mentally, or with chants and movements, they would seek to communicate with animals they used for food so they could learn where they were.

The reason we developed richer communication skills than other animals was because of an innate desire to constantly improve our circumstances. This desire, along with compassion for the welfare of others, compelled us to share information, which in turn required us to describe what we perceived. It was the spiritual impetus of selfishly desiring something better materially and socially, coupled with the practice of sharing what we learned with one another that goaded humans to communicate in ways that changed their body chemistry and led to improvements in their mental ability and communication physiology. Their desires and progressively developing abilities led them to constantly improve their communication skills, and this in turn made it possible for them to work together to create better health, safety and conveniences for all in their group.

One marker of the break of Homo sapiens from other hominin species was the emergence of the use of symbols. Archeologists have found evidence of this in pre-historic jewelry and art. They believe that those who showed

creativity in their use of symbols beat out all the other species to become the only hominin species of today.

Patching together evidence from fossils' DNA found in widely separated archeological sites in Africa, it appears that Homo sapiens interacted with one another as well as with other species whenever ecological conditions allowed groups to move. Their use of symbols sometimes developed separately and sometimes together depending on changes in long weather patterns.

The connecting thread was the regular use of symbols in art which may have led to the reflective insight into cause and effect order that resulted in tool formation and craft skills. It is possible that the tensions produced by periodic group mixing and separation honed their skills of perception and communication, advancing the symbol loving Homo sapiens' brain changes over those of other hominins. (See *Trends in Ecology and Evolution,* by archaeologist Eleanor Scerri).

Professor Kevin Laland, (author of *Darwin's Unfinished Symphony: How Culture Made the Human Mind*) explains that human culture – living in groups, seeking improvements and teaching one another diverse information – formed our anatomy and cognition. Then, when groups reached the threshold of developing agriculture – which allowed a more diverse and secure food source and freed up time for innovation – an explosion of changes followed that accelerated our control over our circumstances and environment.

Clarity of expression is an ongoing human goal. Confucius said the correct use of language is the basis on which sociopolitical order is built. What a noble person conceives he must be able to express accurately to others. A noble person is not vague, but communicates clearly and fully, he said. (A. 13.3) The accurate use of language is something we learn intentionally, because we desire greater clarity in our communications.

Thousands of years ago, some people desired to convey information over distances of space and time and added to their penchant for making tools, crafts and symbolic jewelry the communication of acts in pictures. The pictures of objects and acts became symbols for words. These expanded and developed into symbols that could express thoughts and feelings, as well.

There was a giant leap when an alphabet was created – a few symbols that represented the sounds of verbal language and that could be arranged variously to convey all of the information one could speak. People appreciated that, if they learned these symbols, they could greatly expand the audience with whom they communicated. Economic and medical information were recorded, and courts of law used written records to guide judgments. History and religious information that had previously been transmitted by easy to remember rhymes, were put into writing.

Using symbols, as in art, is something that differentiates us from other animals. The Designer and Creator of the spiritual and material realms often communicates in the universal language of symbols. We may see this communication in dreams or visions, or we might interpret it from coincidences or from events that have a common symbol. The parables Jesus gave may have come from symbols that he perceived in God's communications to him.

According to the Bible, God asks us to give a symbol or sign of acknowledgement and of obedience. This sign is to keep the seventh day each week as a Sabbath, a day of complete rest. The Bible says that this is a signal, or sign, between us and God that we are willing to live by the rules God made. Be still and know that I am God, is what a psalmist perceived God was saying. (Psalm 46:10; 1 Kings 19:11-13)

Why seven days and not six, eight or ten? It might help us understand this symbol if we remember that the moon's phases move through a cycle of 28 days – or 4 times seven. Each phase is usually seven days long. All ancient calendars were lunar calendars. This is part of the natural rhythm of this planet and solar system. When we participate in this rhythm we show respect for, and help to sensitize ourselves to, the Power that designed and created it.

Though spiritual communication is often in symbols, God also puts communications in writing by guiding God-seeking messengers to record what they receive by inspiration. Muhammad said that if the ocean was ink to write God's words, it would be exhausted before the word was exhausted, even if there was another ocean added. (S. 18:109) Jesus said that God's words are food for our spirits. (DT 8:3; MT 4:3-4) In John 6 he identified his teaching as bread/food for our spirits and his example as drink. Because he told us to remember him whenever we bless bread and wine, it is his teaching and example we are charged to remember by daily feeding our spirits through studying his words and life.

No matter how many times we read religious scriptures, we learn from their symbolism. Our experiences and perceptions change constantly and religious scriptures are like a many facetted gem stone that reveals its truths depending on the light which we bring to it.

Isaiah said that if you want to understand God's communications to you, live righteously. When we break the fixed laws God created to govern the spiritual realm, it is an act of rebellion that shuts our spiritual eyes and ears and keeps us from perceiving and interpreting God's communications to us. The Psalmist (34:16) said that God cannot be seen by those who do evil. Muhammad also said that Allah doesn't guide those who do wrong. (S. 28.50) Isaiah (58:1-14, 1:10-20) begged law breakers to change -- so they could discern God's guidance.

In India's religions, one of the techniques for spiritual cleansing is **honesty**. Buddhists train their followers to watch their speech and analyze themselves for motives of untruth and unkindness. In teaching honesty, Confucius said, I don't know how someone who isn't honest manages. A necessary element is missing. (A 2.22)

By your words you will be justified and by your words condemned, is the way Jesus said it. (MT 12:36-37) Like a chemical interaction gone awry, dishonesty distorts what we perceive and how we communicate. The religious the world over hold that we are cleansed spiritually when we practice honesty with ourselves and one another. We must communicate honestly with ourselves and others in order to open a path within us to clearly interpret communications that come to us.

To perceive and interpret God's communications we must be honest, develop spiritual sensitivity by living according to the laws of spiritual nature, and humble ourselves, setting aside regular times when we can be still and open up to being taught and guided by the Great Spirit, the Designer and Creator of the spiritual and material realms.

God is truth/law/purity. God is also alive and omniscient. God already knows all our thoughts, words and deeds. It is OK to be vulnerable and emotionally naked before God. God knows all of our history anyway, and it clears our own communication lines if we don't try to hide it or to justify errors.

Everything we think, say and do communicates to our body chemistry and causes changes in it. Our interactions within our social groups also are like chemistry and cause changes that reverberate far and wide. It is through communication that we shape ourselves and our world.

Like chemistry, some combinations of thoughts, words and acts are toxic, while others are healing. We constantly experiment and learn, through experience and reflection, which communications build peace within ourselves and with others, and which ones devolve into destructive consequences. Like chemistry, there's no way to know all the micro and macro aftereffects of our mix of words, tones, facial expressions and actions. Every expression spews out into other minds and reverberates across time and relationships in near and distant places. We should be careful that the social chemistry we create is constructive.

Teaching is how humans began to develop mental abilities long ago. Teaching others incentivizes us to research more thoroughly and dig more deeply for understanding. It requires us to be more honest and accurate in our communications. This process shapes our communication skills so that, by following our compassionate desire to **educate** others, we find that we simultaneously develop better ways to educate ourselves.

HONESTY

Muhammad said that, other than truth there is only error. (S. 10:32) God created order out of chaos by applying the truth of fixed, eternal laws.

In science, if something has been proved to be true it is called a law. To discover and articulate a scientific truth – a law of the material realm – requires a sense of order, close observation, diligent inquiry, redundant experimentation, inspiration, and the ability to define the law, the process that proves it and the value of its application. There are laws in the spiritual realm as well and, similarly, they can be researched, experimented with and proved to be true.

Pontius Pilate said to Jesus, "Truth, what is that?" (JN 18:38) If we live a life of lies, we cannot perceive or understand valuable truths that would be to our benefit to learn. Being honest with ourselves and others clears our perceptions and makes it easier for us to grasp the intent of invisible order so we can define it and apply it in the form of laws.

Confucius said, the desire of a noble person is truth. He is anxious lest he doesn't find truth. He is not anxious if poverty is his lot. (A. 15.31)

Honesty is different from absolute truth, the kind of eternal truths that constitute laws. Where honesty is concerned we think, speak and behave according to what we believe is true about the material, relationship and spiritual spheres. Nevertheless, being honest about what we believe to be true aids our ability to research and interpret events, as well as to create experiments to prove their causes and to teach what we learn to others.

We look for honesty in our relationships. If you seek to appoint someone as a judge over you, you want him or her to be honest, unbiased and analytical, someone who shows respect for and obedience to the written law and who applies it with wisdom – seeking what is best for those who are involved in disputes. You no doubt want your physician to be honest and to not make you sick so he or she can make money off your treatment. You hope that business owners are honest and that for the sake of enriching themselves they do not sell you products that are dangerous or wasteful. You expect writers and teachers to be honest and to give accurate information and not mislead others to behave immorally or to behave in ways that damage themselves or the community. Of course, everyone depends on their family members to be honest. If dishonesty is found at this intensely personal level it may lead to the breakup of the relationship. Trust is like an egg – once broken it has to be regrown from scratch. We find it difficult to trust people who are dishonest.

According to the Bible, we should speak up if we have information that is of benefit to others. For instance, we are held accountable if we are a witness and we withhold information. (LV 5:1-13) Heeding this, some spiritual leaders have felt compelled to warn their contemporaries and to share what they have learned about spirituality, even when their lives were threatened as a result. In addition, in our efforts to be honest and speak up when we have information that is of benefit to others, we should make life-saving information open source – that is, freely available to all who seek it.

We are compelled, just by living, to express ourselves. However we choose to do that impacts the health of our bodies as well as our relationships. Besides causing specific electrical patterns in our brains, our thoughts, words and acts simultaneously cause chemical releases and reactions throughout our body. In her book, *Molecules of Emotion: The Science Behind Body-Mind Medicine,* Candace Pert, Ph.D., explains how all of our physical systems are inextricably linked in a secondary macro nervous system. Joy, love, anger, stress and depression change our body chemistry. Our choices to be honest or dishonest change our body chemistry, too.

About honesty Pert says there is a physiological reason why honesty reduces stress. When our emotions are at cross purposes our physiologic integrity is altered. This results in a weakened, disturbed psychosomatic network that can lead to stress and to illness.

Honesty also impacts our interpretation of the patterns of events around us. Critical information we deliberately withhold, as well as a lie we tell to ourselves or others, can change how we perceive, interpret and respond to events around us.

Muhammad pointed out that honesty can break up negative patterns of events in our lives and free up our future. (S. 26:221-222) When we are honest it clears up our thinking and we are able to see better ways to respond to others. He also said that we cannot be dishonest with ourselves and be one in purpose with Allah. In order to be compatible with God -- the Designer and Creator of the fixed laws, the eternal truths that govern the spiritual and material realms -- we must be honest.

The religious traditions that have shaped the civilizations of today's world acknowledge the destructive power of gossip and slander, and forbid it. Thousands of years ago, the royal Egyptian petitioner vowed that he had not falsely accused anyone. (19)

Mahatma Gandhi, who led the movement to liberate India from British Colonial rule, insisted that the whole nation practice ahimsa -- the absence of the desire to harm by thought, word or deed -- because only pure means could bring about a pure end. Miraculously, the non-violent, weapons-free Hindus wrested control of their nation out of the grip of the powerful British without a war, using only civil disobedience.

The Buddha described verbal merits as to abstain from lying, rude language, meaningless talk and passing on rumors. In the Noble Eight Fold Path he required purity of speech. The Buddha rejected the notion that it is possible to know what is a true doctrine, and advised his followers to not argue about what spiritual teaching is ultimately true. They are all ideas people have created to suit themselves, he said. Instead, he advised them to not make judgments, but just be and allow others to be. Much of the Buddha's training for initiates involved what to avoid mentally, emotionally, behaviorally and in the world.

Confucius said that a noble person can be counted on to tell the truth. (A. 13.21) In the Ten Commandments we are told that it is a sin to give false witness about others. (DT 5:20) Slander, and lies for financial profit or to deliberately manipulate and mislead others, all diminish those who use them. They cause chemical and spiritual chaos within them in proportion to the magnitude and frequency of their lies. Jesus said that not bearing false witness against others is necessary in order to have eternal life. (MK 10:19) Muhammad urged his followers to ascertain the truth of second hand information and avoid passing on what is false. (S. 49:6)

If someone is dishonest in little, he is dishonest in much, Jesus said. He called the Pharisees hypocrites because they taught one set of rules but lived by another. (MT 23:13-29) He also said that if we aren't honest with money, that transient thing, who will give us what is our very own – meaning our original spiritual skills and powers, and our place with God beyond time and substance. (LK 16:10-13) Honesty must be ingrained in every corner of our lives so we have a "clean" spirit with which to worship God and perceive God's guidance.

The snake is a symbol of lies and liars throughout the Bible. (GN 3:1-5; DT 32:33; Psalm 58:1-5; LK 3:7; MT 23:33; Revelation 12:1-10) It was the lie we told ourselves in the "Garden of Eden" – that we could choose our will over God's will and not be punished for it – that caused us to separate ourselves from God and become entangled with the material realm. To free ourselves from the realm of time and substance and return to our place with God, we must give up lying to ourselves and to others, and live our lives according to eternal truths.

At the end of the book of Revelation (21:5-8) we are told that liars are among those who are denied entrance to Heaven. We cannot create a spiritual rhythm that is compatible with God, and which would allow us to transition back to our original place with our Creator, if we lie to ourselves or to others.

HONESTY EXPERIMENT

When you exercise honesty with yourself and others and show love and respect for God and your neighbor, you are in a position where you may more easily receive God's answers to your specific questions.

Here is an experiment. Write a list of your beliefs and some questions you have about spirituality. Underline the questions. Choose one, and pray during your evening prayers for God to show you the answer. Move your ego aside, be still and leave your mind open to receive God's guidance. If guidance comes at that time, follow that guidance. If not, hold the expectation of an answer in your mind and then retire for the night. The answer may come to you as you waken in the morning, or at some time during the ensuing days.

If it is a complex or painful question, you may be led to steps you have to take before the answer can be revealed to you. Your mind may want an answer, but your spirit may block it because you aren't emotionally ready for it yet. Work through the steps. Keep a journal of parts of the answer that come to you. Honesty is a key that can open a channel in your mind through which to perceive spiritual communication. As you develop your ability to be honest and work through step after step and question after question you will strengthen your communication link with God, and simultaneously your trust that God cares about you personally and seeks to lead you spiritually.

CREATIVITY

The Great Designer and Creator of the universe uses the universal language of symbols to communicate with us. Consider this symbol: first a design was created. Then, as if the Designer was making up rules for a game, laws were created and applied to materials that had been brought about to fulfill the design. Divine Impetus was shown in the

Big Bang and its continuing repercussions, which caused the material realm to develop according to God's design. From this we see God's creativity in the implementation of a design brought about by the deliberate imposition of laws to materials and energies.

We use symbols, too, to express our feelings and discoveries. One early use was by employing symbols and rhythms in poetry. One of the Buddha's earliest teaching manuals was a book of poetry called, *The Book of Eights*. The rhythm and beauty of poetry makes memorization easier. Like a good actor brings Shakespeare's words to life, Buddhist teachers made the meaning of the symbols clear by voice inflections, facial expressions and body movements. They traveled from place to place performing their teaching poetry. *The Book of Eights* spread all over India and beyond, and was popular for centuries.

Teaching by performing poems or songs, as in the Psalms in the Bible and in Hinduism's *Rig Veda*, was a popular way to fix the teaching in an audience's mind. In Hinduism, dance, music, poetry and literature are of great importance and point beyond the material to heighten spiritual experience. The *Rig Veda*, the earliest Hindu scripture, contains over a thousand hymns, poems and mantras.

Though King David broke many of the Bible's laws, had multiple wives and concubines and yet committed adultery and had the woman's husband killed, he did one spiritual thing exceedingly well – he made the Invisible, Living God popular with the Hebrews. He celebrated God publically. He gave God all the credit for his military victories. He also wrote dozens of songs praising and glorifying the One Almighty Ever-Living God, and materially supported those who wrote, sang and spread songs about God. Singing about God impressed the reality and presence of the Invisible God into the hearts and minds of the Hebrews. The Bible's psalms are still read, studied, rehearsed and sung by Jews and Christians these thousands of years after him.

There is no record that Muhammad committed adultery or murder-for-convenience, but Muhammad also did something spiritual exceedingly well. Through much self-denial and prayer, he dictated the book of poetry and spiritual teaching called *The Holy Qur'an*. He described God as light, a light darting across crystal, a star in olive oil that spreads light on light and sheds light on Whomsoever He pleases. (S. 24:35) Before the sun, moon or stars, there was light – the light of God's Spirit and love. *The Holy Qur'an* is so beautiful that many memorize the whole book (about 450 pages) even today. Muhammad said that no one can speak with God except by revelation, or symbol. (S. 42:51)

Jesus' parables were designed to carry spiritual messages. He chose a poetic turn of phrase when he chastised the leaders of his day by saying they strained out gnats but swallowed camels whole -- meaning they obsessed over trivia but made no complaint about blatant law breaking. (MT 23:24) Creativity in language gives us vivid and powerful word pictures.

Confucius was impressed by the ability of the arts to transform human nature. The arts of peace are music, poetry and drawing, or painting, he said. He compiled the famous *Book of Odes* (poetry and songs) of ancient China, which is revered like the Psalms in the Bible. He taught that the Odes cause us to be reflective, and that they teach various social skills. He said they gave him inspiration. (A. 17.9) Confucius also wrote poetry, played the lute and sheng (a polyphonic reed instrument) and loved to listen to music. There is a record that he once sang some of his songs to cheer up his disciples when they were poor and sick. Confucius said that poetic symbolism builds the mind. He said that living virtuously builds character, and music completes the person. (A. 8.8)

The Bible tells us that prophets sometimes acted out symbols. As long as Moses kept his arms raised, the

69

Hebrews had the advantage in a battle. When he tired, others held his arms up so the Hebrews would win. (EX 17:8-13) The Ten Plagues God brought about in Egypt to cause the release of the Hebrews from slavery were symbolic of God's power over Egyptian gods represented by the plagues. (EX 7-11) Jeremiah broke a pot as a symbol that Judah would be broken because of idol worship and injustice. (Jeremiah 19:1-12)

The Bible is full of symbolic stories – such as the Garden of Eden and the Prodigal Son. (GN 3; LK 15:11-24) It is as if our souls remember a universal language of symbols and so we use symbols in stories about our history. Pictures, poetry, stories and music are symbolic and impart more information than their mere expression because of what they cause us to remember, imagine or discover.

We are a type of animal who has within us a spirit that, in some small way, is like the Great Spirit that designed a pattern, created laws and materials and selectively applied the laws to create what It had designed. The reason we can perceive and define invisible laws and use them to create objects for convenience and safety is because something within us is made in the likeness of the One Who made up the design and the laws, and this something is able to connect dissociated symbols and understand their cause and effect order. It is our spirit that is made like this. One could conjecture that it is our seeking spirit that sparks the desire in us to constantly improve our circumstances and ourselves, a desire that activates chemicals, etches pathways, builds networks and develops the wonderful computer that is our brain.

Other animals communicate with sounds, body language and actions. Some bird and mammal species share a common pattern of the pitch and speed of sounds, and can understand one another's communications of fear, hostility, appeasement and submission. Primates can be taught to use sounds, tokens, sign language and touch screens to communicate simple messages to humans, such as music preferences.

We are a more inventive species. We are never satisfied. We are spiritually motivated to constantly desire to improve. As long as we have health, security and materials, we are drawn to reflect, experiment and create crafts, tools, structures and items for convenience and safety. We crave to keep improving on what was made before. At one time we lived in caves, then we moved to tents, then to rock houses, then to wood houses of a wide variety of styles and, more recently, to zero energy homes. We are always seeking to improve our material circumstances – as well as our emotional, relationship and spiritual conditions.

Our spiritual chemistry, if you will, activates creativity. Sharing insights with others through the symbolism of the arts has an impact on our chemistry and etches new pathways in our brains. This enables us to think creatively, compare disassociated events and perceive the invisible cause and effect order of laws.

Writing, made up of symbols, enables us to create a record of our discoveries so that succeeding generations might learn from them and continue to improve. We use the symbols in writing mathematics to aid us in our science communications. Understanding symbols comes from and contributes to our creativity. It makes it possible to communicate what we have learned over time and distances.

Our creativity itself is a symbol that the spirit within us is alive, active and seeking to solve puzzles. With it we see and think symbolically, and this aids us in interpreting God's communications to us.

CREATIVITY EXPERIMENT

A uniquely human skill is that we create art for communication and to give joy to ourselves and others. There is no limit to the kind of art you can create. So, pray about it and then let the Lord lead you – perhaps to reuse an old or found object, or perhaps to develop a new skill. Besides pictures and crafts, art includes songs and music, dance, stories, stage plays and film.

This experiment is to make your own art work that celebrates your experience of a spiritual event. Keep a journal during the days of your creativity, and afterwards evaluate how being deliberately creative gives you new insights into your everyday experiences.

EDUCATION

Confucius is revered as China's Greatest Teacher. He was a professional teacher, and he never refused to teach anyone who sought learning from him. In order to have humanity you must love learning, he said. Otherwise one devolves into frivolity, banditry, brutality, violence and anarchy. (A. 17.8) Someone who cherishes knowledge and continually learns makes a good teacher, he said. (A. 2.11) A fundamental trait of those cultures around the world that have developed out of Confucius' teachings is their strong emphasis on education.

We are egotistical and arrogant when we think we know it all and no longer have anything to learn – that we have "arrived" because of education, status or age. In fact, learning is a lifelong occupation. We should always be humble, ready to learn more and willing to teach those who ask it of us.

Jesus told a story about three men who were given money gifts before their master went to another country for awhile. One man hid his gift and was given a severe punishment when his master returned and demanded an accounting. He was accused of being lazy and wasting the gift he had been given. (MT 25:14-30) This story is symbolic. Jesus told it to point out that everyone is born with their own unique abilities and that while we are on Earth we should use our abilities to engage with the challenges of life and increase our knowledge, skills and strengths.

Over two thousand years ago the Buddha noticed that humans are plagued with feelings of desperation for which we don't understand the source or the cure. Our spirit is aware that we should be feeding it spiritual food and learning spiritual lessons while we are on Earth. However, our conscious mind may not recognize that spiritual food is our need or know how to go about getting it. The Buddha suggested meditation and the denial of emotions and physical desires.

The Buddha was a teacher who composed and performed poetry that explained his philosophy. Abraham taught his whole household the "ways of the Lord." Jesus was an itinerant teacher who carried his message to synagogues, open fields and private dinners – wherever people gathered. After his resurrection, Jesus sent his disciples out to **teach** all nations to obey all that he had commanded them, and to **teach** repentance for the forgiveness of sins. (MT 28:18-20; MK 13:10; LK 24:45-47; Acts 1:8)

In the religions of India, knowledge is one of the Four Paths to liberation from reincarnating into the material realm. It isn't knowledge about worldly things that is needed, but knowledge about how to connect with your spirit, and then with the Spirit that is All-In-All.

Kevin Laland pointed out that, "whereas copying is widespread in nature, teaching is rare, and yet teaching is universal in human societies." Teaching provided the impetus for the development of complex languages, because explicit language was needed for fidelity in transmitting information. Researchers believe this transformed human anatomy and cognition.

In Deuteronomy (11:18-21, 32:45-47) we are told to **teach** children the way of the Lord, and the Law. It is every parent's responsibility to give spiritual guidance to their children. We are responsible for the quality and content of the stimuluses we give to children.

I still remember an argument my parents had when I was about ten years old. My mother was saying it is the letter of the (Biblical) law that is most important. My father insisted it is the meaning, the intent, of the law that is more important. I was still thinking about that when I chose philosophy as my major in college years later. Speak of God and spiritual rules when you are coming and going, when you are sitting and standing, Moses taught. (DT 6:6-7) You never know who may be listening and how it may affect them!

A child's brain is still forming during its first five years. Therefore, it is counter-productive to allow young children to watch violence on television, even violent cartoons, during this time because it leaves the permanent impression on the child's mind that violence is acceptable and that it doesn't carry serious consequences. Hundreds of studies over many decades agree that entertainment violence can lead to increases in aggressive attitudes, values and behavior, particularly in children.

After the age of five or six the child's sense of order and trust should have been established. After age seven the child should be even more able to distinguish between fantasy and reality. Studies have shown that our brain goes through another period of growth and change during our teen years, when our body chemistry is changing from childhood to adulthood. We are especially vulnerable to miscalculations and erratic judgments at this time. Parents, teachers -- and we ourselves -- should be careful about what we feed our mind at every stage of life.

Those who teach us the laws of spiritual nature give us spiritual food and it lights up the spirit within us. Muhammad said that he is a lamp spreading light, a messenger and warner. He said that the Qur'an is a light. (S. 33:45-46, 34:28) He made the Qur'an easy to understand and memorize. It is poetry in Arabic. If some say that he fabricated it, let them produce something like it, he said. (S. 52:33-34) Muhammad told his followers to recite and **teach** the Qur'an. (S. 18:27) He said that those who don't follow his teachings will be drawn to follow their own lusts. (S. 28:50) If Allah does not guide you, there is no way to the goal, he said. (S. 42:46) A psalmist caught sight of this concept and wrote, if God does not build the house, in vain do the builders toil. (Psalm 127:1-2)

Jesus also said that he is the light of the world and that his teachings are spiritual food for our souls. (JN 8:12, 6:27-35, 40, 52-63) Jesus said that those who don't commit to his teachings are condemned because they love darkness. (JN 3:17-21, 8:51)

Abraham, who had chosen to seek and submit to God, taught his family and household (which included his slaves) to seek God's will and follow it. His interpretation of religion was a radical change from the religions and cultures of his time, where people sought to coerce the powers in the spiritual realm to further their own selfish goals. (GN 18:19, 14:14, chapters 12-25:11) It is significant that Abraham taught his interpretation to others instead of just living it. The act of teaching, in itself, is critically important to our mental development and this teaching, in particular, is critically important to our spiritual development.

God didn't rescue the Hebrew slaves out of Egypt just to be Mr. Nice Guy. He had a job for them to do for Him. Their mission was to be a nation of priests who would **teach** the world (beginning in Canaan) about the One Invisible Ever-Living God, Maker of Heaven and Earth, the laws God created that govern spiritual nature, and the transformative spiritual power of submission to God's personal daily guidance. (DT 29:9-14; Joshua 8:32-35; Psalm 22:27; Isaiah 49:1-6, 66:18-24; Micah 4:1-4)

Over the centuries, however, many Hebrews succumbed to peer pressure from the people in the nations around them and participated in idol worship and its associated religious and sexual practices. Then, after returning from their punishing deportation to Babylon, the Jews focused on keeping the laws, but forgot their broader mission to teach about God to the world. Jesus came to remind them that they were supposed to be like salt – cleansing and purifying the nations – and like a light on a stand that gives light to the whole (world) house. When their leaders rejected Jesus' interpretation of the intent of the laws written by Moses, and reminders of their mission, Jesus said God would choose others to carry out the mission. (MT 22:1-14)

EDUCATION EXPERIMENT

We learn when we teach. Your experiment is to research, write about and speak out about a favorite subject, something you are passionate and want to learn more about. Plan to prepare a five minute talk about your subject.

Then consider how these same skills of research, writing and speaking, or debating, can be used to teach yourself and others more about a religious theme. Look for opportunities to do this at your place of worship or in your community.

RESEARCH: Invest in books about your favorite subject. Collect articles as you see them in newspapers and magazines. Check the Internet and Wikipedia for background information. Pray for guidance and write notes as you are inspired. One technique is to cut 8 ½ by 11 inch paper into four parts. Write one sentence on each part and arrange them to form paragraphs. Another technique is to write an outline of main questions or ideas you want to cover in your paper, and let the outline guide your research.

Your writing should aim to follow a pattern. First, you might give history and background about the topic, to lay a foundation for your audience. Then explain why what you are going to say is important to the community – its moral or value base. This is the skeleton of your project. Next, flesh it out with your research, interpretations and suggestions. What have you learned from your research, and how do you intend to use it? Finally, draw the reader in by suggesting what the reader can do to use the information and/or find out more about the topic.

WRITING: Writing a poem about each aspect of your subject can reveal depth and flavor in your topic. Writing poetry helps to cut away fluff and condense ideas to their essence. It can lead you to see symbols and similarities which you would otherwise miss.

SPEAKING: Practice out loud – over and over. Revise for clarity. Revise for power points. Revise for entertainment. As you read your paper out loud, imagine your audience and questions they might have about what you have written.

*****

If you teach a class, you can observe the power that teaching gives to learning. Pair students and have them teach each other in turn a single lesson. Then test them on that lesson. This brief exercise will help anchor the lesson in their minds, because in order to teach it to their partner they have to reflect on it and understand it themselves.

CHAPTER FOUR

LOVE

Love is absolute. God loves us, the Psalmist says, whether we are in heaven or hell, whether we run away all day or hide all night. (Psalm 139) No matter where we are in our spiritual journey, no matter what we think or do, we will never be outside of God's love for us. Love is everlasting, a fundamental force in the spiritual realm.

Because of the abiding love of the Great Spirit, those spirits who rebelled against It were not extinguished but only put in "time out" -- a place where we can experience the repercussions of our choices, recognize our errors and take the actions necessary to demonstrate repentance with complete love, obedience and submission to our Creator.

It was out of great love that God created the material realm – the entire universe, from its core to its vast stretching reaches – with precision, rhythm and cause and effect order to protect and communicate with free will souls who had chosen their will over God's will. Out of love God designed the material realm to provide all our needs while we are here, while also providing a venue within which our souls might recognize their mistakes and rectify them.

Muhammad reminds us often that God is the Cherisher of human souls and is oft forgiving. Nevertheless, God does not scorn the victims of human error. By the laws for the spirit that God created, those who deliberately cause injustice and tragedy simultaneously set themselves up to be corrected in their current or future life, until they also balance spiritually and choose to live by the laws that govern spiritual nature.

The perfect **order** designed into the material realm is a symbol of God's **loyalty**. It provides a foundation for the security we need to reach out in faith so we can learn, change and grow. As we build loyalty and order into our relationships we help each other have an extra measure of security so we can admit mistakes, change and grow spiritually. When, in addition, we give one another the emotional grounding of **forgiveness**, we encourage the flowering of abilities with which to meet material and spiritual needs.

God's loyalty is endless. Deep in our souls we are aware of God's loyalty to us, and this draws us subconsciously to desire loyalty in our relationships and to learn how to give loyalty back to others, and to God. We show love to God when we seek God loyally. We show respect by living within the limits of the laws God created. We further our spiritual mission by showing loyalty and respect to others and helping them learn about God and the laws of spiritual nature.

Loyalty and forgiveness are part of God's loving nature which some call grace, and are also traits found in our own nature. We show love by being loyal even to those with whom we disagree, giving necessary material aid and the moral support of good guidance. The Bible tells us we should give support in emergency situations, even to enemies. God told the Hebrews to love foreigners because the Hebrews were once foreigners in Egypt. (DT 10:19)

Some might ask, if God has eternal love for us, then doesn't He accept us back to His place no matter how many laws of spiritual nature we break? But God's endless love isn't a free pass to commit whatever selfish, unjust or brutal behavior we may find convenient at any given time. Sin (to "miss the mark") is rebellion against God and rejection of the laws that govern spiritual nature. When we sin we turn away from, and refuse to listen to and obey, God. The laws of both material nature and spiritual nature are fixed. When we break the laws of either realm we hurt ourselves; we take ourselves out of sync with each realm. God goes on loving us, but we damage ourselves spiritually when we break a law of spiritual nature. It throws us out of spiritual balance and keeps us from being compatible with God, Who is Spirit, so that we are unable to return to live eternally with God. (JN 4:24)

God's love for us is shown in His loyalty to us. In His great love for us God never gives up trying to bring each soul to recognize His presence, His intimate concern and the way to return to live eternally with Him. When painful things happen to us it is because we, or those with whom we interact, have broken a law of either the spiritual or material realms. If we intently seek comfort and guidance from God at those times, it is forthcoming.

God showed love for the descendants of Abraham by rescuing them from the grip of the powerful nation of Egypt where they had become slaves, protecting them in the barren wilderness after they rebelled against Him, helping them expel idol worshippers and the sexually immoral from the land to which they were led, and helping them settle in a country they could call their own. When they were disloyal to Him, He showed love by correcting them, speaking through messengers to guide them back to Him, and restoring them after they repented. God had a mission for the descendants of Abraham and the converts to their religion, and He guided, chastised and protected them so they had the opportunity to fulfill that mission.

Because we have free will, we also have the ability to express the lack of love, such as when we renege on responsibilities, tell lies, scorn or spread rumors about others, cheat one another, commit murder, take excessive revenge or make choices because of prejudice instead of taking the time to investigate and choose fairly. We can choose against love, or we can respond to life's challenges with loyalty, forgiveness, compassion and an attitude that seeks understanding.

New mistakes and injustices happen all the time, setting up cycles of negative thoughts and behavior. We should always ask for God's guidance in how to respond to injustice and brutality, and take serious matters to a court of law so the pain caused to one is not caused to others.

While we may forgive wrong doing, we should keep in mind that forgiveness is not trust. In order to avoid being re-victimized, we need to exercise **caution** in interacting with those who have broken trust with us. Confucius told us to love everyone, but to develop friendships with the virtuous. (A. 1.6) Jesus told us to be perfect, and to love even our enemies, but to let the (spiritually) blind lead those (who choose to be spiritually) blind. (MT 5:44-48, 15:14)

So, the question arises as to how to show love for one another when spiritual laws are broken and, in extreme situations, how to show love for those who try to lead society to validate and promote law breaking behavior. They may do good things in other areas of their lives, but because they are in open rebellion against the laws that govern spiritual nature, and because they seek to advise youth and others to indulge in law breaking behavior, they should be reprimanded and, Jesus would say, shunned. (MT 18:15-17)

Confucius advised that if someone is arrogant and mean, all his good qualities count for nothing. (A. 8.11) Likewise, through Ezekiel God said that if a righteous man sins, all his righteousness is counted for nothing. (Ezekiel 18:24) To reward and honor people who we know are breaking the laws of spiritual nature (such as those who change society's laws in order to validate sexual deviancy or to legalize murder, theft, recreational addictive substances, prejudice or injustice) is to encourage impressionable youth to follow their un-reprimanded example. It also does not show love to the law breakers, because their errors will stick to them like glue in their current life as well as when they are evaluated when they transition into the spiritual realm after death, and will still have an impact on them in a future life.

Like the unruly child who is separated from the class and must sit in a corner, some members of society disrupt society when they don't follow the Fundamental Laws. So, it is a benefit to them and, by example, to others when they are shunned until they exhibit better behavior.

We must always treat law breakers respectfully, and be ready to acknowledge and encourage any efforts they make to repent. Though they be shunned, we should make sure their emergency and basic needs are met. In treating others as we would want to be treated, we should respond to them with respect and calmly offer them opportunities to change and to make restitution where that is needed.

Like a doctor who gives a patient life-saving advice that the patient doesn't follow, or a parent who gives a child moral guidance that the child rebels against, after we do the best we know how to help others, sometimes we have to let go and just love them and comfort them when they get hurt. If you are living by the Fundamental Laws and teaching your loved ones to live by the laws and they rebel, shunning them until they show evidence of repentance over time can give an example of repercussions for law breaking that will lead many others to choose God's way over their own carelessness or selfishness. In the event that the rebel devolves into worse behavior, though one may be lost many may be saved by the example of their pattern of behavior and its repercussions. Each one of us is on our own spiritual journey, and we need to discover and resolve the reasons we hurt ourselves and others. Emergency support should be given, but honors, enhancements, entertainment and companionship withheld.

"God loves you, do what you want," has been the tempter's mantra since the Garden of Eden. "Throw yourself off the parapet; God loves you," Jesus heard the tempter say.

"Heaven is a free gift no matter how you live," is the current version. In the Bible, God said He would tempt us with a wonder worker who tells us to not live by God's rules. (DT 13:2-6) It is always the same lie. It misrepresents God's love as a weak, anything goes, comfort blanket. Instead, God's love is firm, just, always ready to help us learn spiritual lessons so we may succeed in returning to love and submission to God and to living eternally in God's place beyond time and substance -- a place where there is no pain or sorrow, hunger or thirst.

If out of love you pray for someone's spiritual development, you may subconsciously lead yourself to be an opportunity for the person to grow spiritually – by becoming ill or injured or otherwise dependent, for example. But the person may not rise to the occasion and use the opportunity for the growth that could develop from it. Each person's spiritual weaknesses are their own to work out with God. We must be cautious about our interpretations of spiritual needs.

Muhammad said that no one can bear another's burden. (S. 53:38) In the Bible it is said that the child is not to be put to death for the sins of the parent, nor the parent for the sins of the child. (DT 24:16)

The best course may be to attend to your own spiritual growth and, when appropriate, to give suggestions, observations, literature and other kinds of opportunities that may help others with theirs. Always ask God in prayer for the best ways to interact with others that will aid spiritual development. We all have spiritual lessons to learn. That's why we are here. We should work together to support one another while we each grope through the maze of life to prepare for spiritual rebirth.

Jesus said to not give pearls to pigs (unrepentant prostitutes) or holy things to dogs (homosexuals). These are those who are in self-justified rebellion against God's guidance. Nevertheless, he said that prostitutes and tax collectors who repented would go to heaven before the arrogant and hypocritical, law-proclaiming religious leaders. (MT 21:28-32) It all starts with repentance. Then forgiveness and guidance for how to develop spiritual balance is forthcoming. That's the power of love.

Jesus reached out to those despised by the elite, healed Gentiles as well as Jews, taught love of neighbors, fidelity in marriage, patience in oppression and complete love for God. He taught that God wants all to be shown love and to be taught the laws that transform every life from the desperation of chaos to the **joy** and sweetness of spiritual order.

LOYALTY

Loyalty is meant to be pure. It becomes ingrained in us before we can even speak the word. Through the continuous loyalty of our parents we develop layers of essential emotional stability. Interrupted mothering before the age of five, as well as traumatic early childhood experiences, have been shown to be factors that sometimes lead to juvenile delinquency and life course crime. The spiritual nourishment of loyalty is something every child needs as much as they need good quality food for their bodies.

After being nourished with loyalty throughout early childhood, we are prepared to give it back to our family, friends, school, community, sports teams and country. Some expand their loyalty to include Earth. They arrange to live sustainably and be good stewards of our home planet.

Confucius said that filial piety is the root from which moral behavior grows. Children who respect, honor and care for their parents will be free from pride and insubordination. This practice will prepare them to be of service to society and contribute to their community. If one disagrees with parents, one should do it respectfully, he said. (A. 4.18)

Confucius stressed that balance is needed in loyalty, and that both parents and the government should give the aid needed so children are prepared to assume their care giver and citizen roles when they are adults.

One of the Ten Commandments in the Bible bids us to be loyal to our parents. We should help them when we are old enough to do so, and contribute to their well-being. (EX 20:12) Muhammad concurred. He said that God urges us to show gratitude to our parents and to help them meet their needs as we are able. (S. 31:14, 46:15-16)

In the Bible we see that loyalty is tested. Noah was shown how to survive a great flood, but after it abated he had to face a barren land and learn to eat bread grains. Abraham received a promise of blessings from God, but then he was guided to prepare to sacrifice his youngest son. God rescued the Hebrew slaves out of the grip of the powerful Egyptians, but then they experienced hardship to see if they would be faithful to God. When Jesus was baptized he received commendation, but then he was sent to a barren place and tested for 40 days. Early Christians received the blessings of Jesus' teachings and example, but then they were driven from their homes and tortured, testing their loyalty to the spiritual gift they had been given. Today we experience many miracles and blessings, including easily available religious scriptures and teachings. We also are daily tested with distractions, false advice, injustice, dangers and tragedies.

While the desire for loyalty is part of our spiritual nature, being loyal is also a free will choice. Throughout life we are tempted, threatened and given false advice to test our loyalty to friends and family, and to God. (DT 8:2-6, 13:1-5) Living by the laws that govern the spiritual realm and seeking daily guidance from our Creator helps us negotiate life's many dimensions of tests and stay on course with loyalty to others and to God.

All major religions teach the power and importance of loyalty. Confucius taught that loyalty is the first – the most important -- principle. (A. 1.8, 9.25) In the religions of India, the only way to achieve liberation from reincarnation is to complete one of the Four Paths of liberation, which requires loyalty to the disciplines of that path.

Jesus said we should seek to have a "single eye" – that is, to be one in thoughts, words and actions with our soul's innate desire to return to God. (MT 6:22-23) One way we work to develop that single way of seeing is by preparing for and protecting our ability to be loyal to others.

Developing a single eye in the marriage relationship makes it easier for both partners to achieve their spiritual goals. Virginity is a token of loyalty. To remain sexually pure before marriage and give yourself only to your spouse, learning about the beauty and mystery of sex with one another, strengthens the respect you have for each other. (DT 22:13-21)

Muhammad taught a way of life that requires loyalty to God, morality, family and the form of government that protects the faith of its people. In Muslim countries there is no separation between religion and family, or religion and state. The government is expected to be loyal and to protect the faith of its people. The people are expected to be loyal to God and one another, and to their government.

Muhammad said that it is better to marry a believing slave than an unbeliever. (S. 24:32-33) The Biblical law also forbids intermarriage of the God-centered with idol worshippers. (EX 34:12-16, 21:7-8; DT 7:1-4) Marrying within one's religion makes it easier to retain spiritual focus and remain loyal to one's religious values. It is useful for the religious to offer social opportunities that include those who are single so they have the opportunity to meet potential marriage partners of their faith.

The practice of a married couple being loyal to one another through career challenges, parenting responsibilities, health issues and other stresses enriches them spiritually and helps them learn skills they need to stay loyal to God. Adultery -- sometimes engaged in for revenge or to avoid talking out problems -- is expressly forbidden in all three Abrahamic religions as well as in the *Egyptian Book of the Dead.* (12; S. 17:32; EX 20:14; LV 18:20; MT 19:9) It comes under the rule to avoid lust in the teachings of Confucius, the Buddha and the religions of India.

Muhammad said that everything is made in pairs that we may receive instruction. (S. 51:49) The Bible tells us we are made to be helpmates to one another, and that male and female are made to be together. (GN 2:18-24; MT 19:3-6) Marriage is an opportunity to develop spiritual strength through loyalty. Cheating on one's spouse comes from, as well as exacerbates, spiritual weakness.

Nevertheless, if a marriage is dangerously unworkable divorce is allowed, according to teachings in all three of the Abrahamic faiths. (MT 19:9-11; DT 24:1-4) Muhammad said that if a wife fears cruelty or desertion they may divorce. When people divorce, he advised, God hears both sides. (S. 65:1-4, 4:128-130)

Our Creator expects communication and loyalty from us. The first commandment in the Ten Commandments is that God is One and we must have no gods before the One God. (EX 20:3-6) To make anything in life – be it career, family, money, a person, a country or anything else – more important than our respect, love for, obedience and submission to the all-pervading Living Spirit that designed, created and sustains the spiritual and material realms, is idol worship. (DT 5:6-7, 10:20, 30:19-20, 4:39-40, 10:12-13) We are expected to be loyal to God, to be obedient to the rules God created for the spiritual and material realms, and to seek communication and guidance from our Creator.

Through His messengers, God has instructed us to remember Him throughout each day   This is an expression of our loyalty. In the same way that we think about a loved one from time to time throughout the day, we should remember God. In the Bible we are told to wear a bracelet with the First Law – the law to be loyal to God – on it, and to put tassels on the four corners of our "mantle" (blanket) so we remember God all through the night. (NU 15:37-41; DT 6:4-9) According to the Qur'an, regular prayers are required. (S. 17:78) Just as God is loyal to us and constantly present with us, we must develop the ability to keep God in mind and be loyal to God.

LOYALTY EXPERIMENT

During the seven days of Passover -- a spring festival that begins the 15th day after the new moon closest to the Spring Equinox and that commemorates the Hebrews' escape from Egypt (and that coincides with spring planting festivals around the world) -- the longer, deeper Omer "fast" begins. During the 49 days of the Omer we shouldn't eat any grain (some read grass) foods.

As we take a leap of faith and exercise this deep commitment, the self-discipline required by this diet strengthens our spirit's muscle. As with other experiments of spiritual nature, when we give back some of what we have in the material realm – in this case, our time, attention and some food pleasures -- God guides us to experience His presence and guidance – gifts from the spiritual realm.

The Omer is the amount of time between the "morrow after the Sabbath" during Passover week and the Feast of First Fruits, the second of the three festivals that the Bible says we should celebrate for all time. (Passover is the first required festival, and the harvest festival in the autumn, Succoth, is the third.) The Feast of First Fruits starts the morning after the last day of the Omer, on the 50th day. It was after observing the Omer that Jesus' disciples were imbued with the "Spirit from on high." Christians call the day Pentecost, which comes from the Greek word that means fifty.

Keeping the Omer diet is one of the perpetual laws and is given in Leviticus 23:4-5, 9-16. When we practice this discipline we must not eat grain foods (such as wheats, barley, rye, rice, oatmeal, millet and corn) during the seven weeks before the Feast of First Fruits. Some interpret the word to mean grass foods. Using that interpretation would include sugar, as well as some green leafy vegetables and spices.

Archaeologists have found a 10th century B.C. Middle East calendar etched in clay that records the agricultural year. There it is noted that the harvest date for wheat is in the month we call May, which would be at the end of the Omer. The harvest date for barley is a month earlier, but this is not the preferred bread grain. The festival comes after the wheat harvest.

In the Bible we are told to count each day of the Omer. As Christians count Advent before Christmas, Jews count the Omer. You could mark off each day on your calendar and add the Omer number. Counting each day helps you remember to keep the diet, even if food containing grains is offered to you. During each week of the Omer, set aside an offering in proportion to God's blessings to you. Give the offering at the Feast of First Fruits. (DT 16:9-10)

Grains now make up ten of the fifteen most common foods we eat. It wasn't always so. Eating grass and grain foods may have begun with Noah after the Great Flood. (GN 9:1-3) Since that time, human life spans have become increasingly shorter. The Omer diet gives us a chance each year to cleanse our bodies of the effects of grains and turn back the clock a little on the aging process.

The first two or three years that you keep this seven week diet you may actually be able to feel an internal "scrubbing" sensation in your veins that moves from one part of your body to another. Don't be alarmed. The sensation will stop at the end of the Omer. The first three or four days of the diet are the most difficult, as your body adjusts to withdrawing from foods you normally eat.

To keep a grain and grass free diet for 49 days takes some preparation. Imagine being without bread, pasta, cereal, corn, rice, sugar and more for seven weeks. What would you eat? You can eat organic meat, fish, eggs, dairy products (but not cheese, since some varieties are made using grain) fruits, vegetables, nuts, pumpkin and squash seeds, black tea, coffee, date sugar and maple syrup (no stevia).

This diet includes a wide variety of beans, peas and lentils. Powdered garbanzo beans with tahini and a little lemon juice and grated garlic can be cooked into a vegetable stuffing or dip.

I wouldn't recommend mushrooms, which are a fungus that cleans the ground.

Organic butter and peanut or coconut oil may be used to oil cooking pans or to add to vegetables. Common condiments are garlic, onion, salt and horseradish. Keep in mind that ground up spices, as well as other foods in powdered form, may contain fillers that are not listed on the label and that would compromise the diet.

Dried and frozen fruit, oven baked pudding with whole eggs and no cornstarch, as well as fruit and vegetable drinks are fine for the diet. If drinking milk, try to find milk that has not had good bacteria removed (a practice used to extend the shelf life of milk).

You should also drink plenty of pure water. Water that has been filtered and then boiled for 5 or 10 minutes may be better than some brands of spring water.

If at all possible, always use organic foods, and wash all fresh foods with warm water. Peel what can be peeled, in the event the produce was sprayed or dipped in a chemical to extend its shelf life. If you eat mechanically separated nuts or seeds you might want to bake them at low heat for 10 minutes in order to remove the chemical involved in the process. Avoid all chemical additives during the Omer diet.

The Omer diet is an exercise in loyalty. If we can't even be loyal during a 49 day diet, how can God trust us to be loyal for eternity? Counting each day reminds us to be loyal. If you do break with the diet accidentally, start over from day one and try again.

The Omer Diet leads to a joyful conclusion. At the beginning of the diet, write down any illnesses you have. By keeping this diet loyally, you get a big reward at the end when you are able to strike through those health issues that have been overcome.

ORDER

Order is complete. The material realm is guided by a specific design from the smallest nanoparticle to the largest galaxy.

It will never happen that laws will be drawn to materials to create glass, wiring, metal, propulsion fuel, etc. and arrange these objects to create an airplane, on their own. Someone must design the airplane, impose laws on materials and bring the specific, appropriate parts together to form the plane. Laws exist and materials exist but in order for a complex, functioning object to exist there must be a design and the impetus to apply laws to materials to bring about the design. Whose impetus created the laws, the materials and the design for this interdependent cosmos and the Earth?

Primitive people were intimate with nature and knew the orderly movements of stars, planets, the moon, water tides, plant growth, animal habits and human development. The question arose, how did order come to be applied to the materials in nature? Ancient religions usually began their creation stories by explaining how order was imposed on chaos.

Having had experiences of spiritual communication, the ancients imagined that gods in the spiritual realm caused order. Creation stories from all over the world depict battles fought by gods to conquer chaos and impose order. The Bible also tells us that God imposed order on chaos. (Job 38 and 39, 9:13 TNJB)

In India's religions, dharma is the sacred truth, or order, that supports the universe, society, religion and personal duty. "Hindu Dharma" refers to the Hindu way of life, sacrifices to the gods, virtue, rules and duties. These make up the responsibilities one has to one's self and to the environment and is one of human nature's Four Goals (along with pleasure, wealth and salvation).

For Confucius, balance within the individual, the family and society maintains order in the cosmos. Confucius was heavily influenced by ancient Taoism, which taught the spiritual unity of everything in the material realm. Confucius taught that loyalty to family and government, humility, respect and reciprocity (the Golden Rule) are forces that bring about order and balance within us, spread out into society, and impact the world of nature.

This concept is also brought up in the Bible, where Jeremiah complained that because of idol worship and (sexual) wickedness by those who should have known better the rain was withheld and crops failed. (Jeremiah 3:2-3) The world of material nature was impacted because humans had chosen against the laws of spiritual nature.

If material nature was brought about so that certain elements in spiritual nature would have a venue within which to work out their destiny, then perhaps the two realms, in certain ways, interact.

Logos, translated from the Greek as "word," was understood by the Greeks to mean the divine reason that orders the cosmos (i.e., Law). John 1:1 in the Bible could be read as, "In the beginning was the Law and the Law was God." This would make it logical that, "all things were made by Him," refers to God. Verse 14, which is translated as, "the word was made flesh," is where theologians interpret that Jesus was the Law Incarnate. The meaning here is that Jesus understood spiritual order, or law, and taught it.

The Greeks carried the idea of order into their daily discourse where, under the light of logic (a discipline of orderly methods and techniques) they examined information and ideas to determine whether they were correct or incorrect. Interestingly, it is reported that the Buddha, also, would take apart every problem and reconstruct it in logical order with its intent and value articulated.

Order is essential for emotional well-being. A child's brain continues to develop between birth and five years of age. During this time it is essential that the child have an environment that is predictable and dependable, with reliable nourishment and safety. This is a time when children want to hear the same story again and again, and they ask the same questions again and again. This predictability – this redundant order – is one way the child develops trust. Along with loyalty and respect, trust is a component in the spiritual equation that develops our conscience. (Another reason that children may ask "why" again and again is because they want other related information but don't know how to ask for it.) As we grow and encounter the various challenges of life, our spiritual and emotional foundation of conscience gives us the security and confidence to think creatively and find solutions to the problems we encounter. When trust is severely broken in early childhood, we often find dysfunctional and violent teens and adults.

Severe dis-order at any stage of life can cause mental illness. The moral inconsistencies of war, for instance, where soldiers may be forced to act against laws that govern spiritual nature, can result in Post-Traumatic Stress Disorder.

All societies require order in the form of laws and systems so that groups of people can function together to have safety, health and conveniences, as well as to have opportunities to grow mentally, emotionally and spiritually. A society's laws are best crafted and enforced by those who developed a firm conscience during their early years and who carry their expectation for fairness and order into their adult life.

Our ability to think creatively and define cause and effect order has led us to be able to use some of the invisible laws that govern the material realm to create objects and systems to greatly enrich our lives. Because of their sense of order, scientists may pluck disassociated symbols of order from nature and intuit the laws they symbolize.

Dr. J. Bronowski (author of *Science and Human Values*) observed about Isaac Newton that he grasped that the force of gravity that reaches to the tree top might also reach beyond Earth endlessly into space. If so, then gravity would be what holds the moon in its orbit. He calculated the force from Earth that would hold the moon and compared it with the force of gravity at tree height. The two forces agreed. Two unrelated events caught in the mind by their similarity of order revealed a rule about a broader field of order in the material realm.

Scientists today are collecting vast amounts of data in an effort to understand nature's deep, pervasive connectivity. The danger is that they will use this information for economic goals, blind to the deeper, inextricably linked micro and macro systems that protect our planet as it constantly adjusts to changes. All the data in the world will not give them all the answers they need because, besides data, Earth has an intrinsic rhythm in its layered, networked and organically developed systems which are always in motion and are impacted – like the butterfly effect – by small changes as well as large. Human knowledge is not great enough to grasp the infinite after-effects for every action that forces nature against its millennia of organically developed order. There are subtle, powerful repercussions a single change can cause.

Some scientists are in the process of breaking links and systems which other scientists warn will create a cascade of problems they can't anticipate – with no way to reverse the damage. We must show respect for the delicate multidimensional order God created. Trying to re-organize genes, atoms and nanoparticles to serve our selfish purposes could kill us before we have digested the evidence of the destructive power of those actions.

Working with, instead of against, the laws of material nature is an aid to helping us be more sensitive to the order inherent in spiritual nature.

Laws are true, otherwise they are theories. Jesus said the truth will set us free. Recognizing the cause and effect order of spiritual nature and proving to ourselves the validity of the laws that govern the spiritual realm helps us better understand what is true about our own spiritual nature and about the Great Spirit that designed and created us. This gives us incentive to live the way we must to return to our place beyond time and substance where we will live eternally in beauty, peace and joy without material needs or concerns. In this way, truth sets us free.

When we better understand the order of spiritual nature, we can better articulate the laws that govern us and apply them conscientiously to facilitate bringing order within ourselves that can spread out to our society and help us create a sustainable economic system, international peace and sustainable environmental practices.

Muhammad said that Allah created the Heavens and the Earth for just ends, and in order that each soul may find the recompense of what it has earned, and none of them be wronged. (S. 45:22) The order in the universe is a symbol of God's loyalty, dependability and solidarity. Though we have turned away from God, our Creator still loves us and, through the symbolism of the sustaining cause and effect natural world around us, cues us that invisible laws also govern the spiritual world within us, and that wherever an intelligent, free will spirit may be in the universe we can use this knowledge to find our way back to God.

ORDER EXPERIMENT

Many of the world's most accomplished scientists were musicians. The astronomer Ptolemy wrote *Harmonica,* on the mathematics of music. The mathematician Pythagoras wrote about music and universal harmony. Johannes Kepler, who wrote laws of planetary motion, also wrote *The Harmony of the World and Music of the Spheres.* Descartes, who developed methodological skepticism and the scientific method, wrote, *The Compendium of Music.* Isaac Newton equated the color spectrum and musical pitches in his treatise, *Optiks.* Galileo played the keyboard and lute. Michelangelo was a lute player. Max Planck, who originated the quantum theory, composed music, and played the cello and piano. Albert Einstein played piano, viola and violin. Thomas Edison played piano. When we tune in to the order inherent in communicating through the symbolism of rhythmic sounds, it leads us to appreciate cause and effect order wherever we find it.

Daniel J. Levitin in, *This is Your Brain on Music: the science of a human obsession,* tells us that, "Music may be *the* activity that prepared our pre-human ancestors for speech communication and for the very cognitive, representational flexibility necessary to become human.... It involves a precision choreography of neurochemical release and uptake between logical prediction systems and emotional reward systems."

Musical instruments have been discovered that are 60,000 years old, and cave etchings of wind instruments and musicians are much older. Music has helped create the human culture, and has helped develop the human brain.

This experiment is to learn to play a musical instrument in order to help further develop your sense of order.

If you already know how to play an instrument, an additional way to deepen your sense of order is by learning mathematics. The numbers and signs are just symbols. Learn the symbols and the "rules of the game" for a type of mathematics you don't already know and it will help you further develop your sense of order.

Teaching young children to use an abacus will help them learn a sense of order. The beads always give the correct answer when they are properly used.

Developing a sense of order will help you see the order in the world in unrelated events and increase your spiritual ability to creatively solve problems.

CAUTION

Caution is real. It is something we often learn through painful trial and error. Toddlers learn to walk carefully after bumping into things and falling over. They learn what "hot" means by touching a forbidden oven door. As we grow older we continue to learn, through trial and error, how to be cautious.

We may sometimes act impulsively out of fear, depression or sudden joy, but nature's fixed laws do not bend to our emotions. Caution is a brake on our free will. It slows us, and sometimes stops us. It is how we try to protect ourselves and our loved ones. We choose it – or we don't.

When Jesus was in the wilderness and tempted to put God to the test by throwing himself off a high place, he quoted Deuteronomy 6:16 (and see 4-19) saying, "You shall not put the Lord your God to the test." (MT 4:7) We should not presume that a perceived threat, promised blessings, or even a mission that we have received, is an excuse to act irresponsibly.

In order to not be victimized by others we should exercise caution and listen carefully to what people say. Someone who speaks in favor of legalizing addictive drugs, may be signaling a lack of self-control and may someday use the influence of drugs to put you in danger. Someone who tells secrets about someone else, may be planting lies to manipulate your opinion against that person. Someone who is in favor of liberal sexual practices, may disrespect their same or the opposite gender and may someday exploit or assault you. Someone who rejects God and/or accountability on the spiritual side of life, may not exercise a moral brake on their behavior and may be prone to justifying behavior that is illegal by civil law and that puts you and the community in danger. Listening for the message behind the message is a technique of caution.

We also exercise caution in our relationships. Whether within families or between nations, diplomatic skills are a way to be cautious in speech and behavior so we do not incite violence. The sooner diplomacy is learned, the less likely we are to be perpetual victims. Force may sometimes be necessary, but it can be a very destructive way to achieve a goal.

The Buddha advised us to not want anything, even our opinions, if we would be safe from those who would attack us verbally or physically.

Muhammad said we should be cautious and not befriend those who flatter us but who reject spiritual truths. He said that if you work with them they will cause you to act treacherously. They want influence over your works and words so they can make you turn to error, he said. He identified unbelievers as those who are steeped in self-glory, and who create separation by selfishness. (S. 9:34, 2:79, 38:2, 60:1-2, 3:149, 5:51)

Both the Bible and the Qur'an warn us to not marry those who deny the One God. Muhammad went further and said to not associate with those who reject God, because they will influence you to stray away from God. Confucius said to love all people, but befriend the virtuous. Jesus said to leave alone those who reject his teachings. (MT 15:12-14) The Bible warns that if we condone wrong doing we will be drawn into the punishment that naturally accrues to those who break the laws that govern spiritual nature. (NU 33:55-56; DT 12:29-31, 6:14-15) These are all ways that we are warned to be cautious.

We should be careful to not pass along rumors or lies about others. (LV 19:16; EX 20:16) The Buddha recognized tale-bearing and frivolous talk as demerits. Don't give false witness or join a multitude to execute justice without a trial, we are warned in the Bible and the Qur'an. (EX 23:1-2; S. 49:6) Since we are held accountable for what we believe and how we act, it is a good idea to take the time to investigate matters thoroughly and seek guidance in prayer before forming an opinion.

Jesus cautioned us to be as wise as serpents, but as gentle as doves. The serpent is a symbol the Bible uses for lies and liars. We should be wise to the ways of liars and those who con others, without responding in kind. Jesus expects us to discern between those who have been spiritually awakened and those still in self-justified rebellion, and to be especially cautious in interacting with rebels. He told his disciples to move when persecuted. He often moved to avoid abuse and capture, until God directed him to allow it. (MT 10:11-15; JN 11:53-54)

Caution is also a way we show love to our family, community and the Earth. Not everything we can do is what we should do. Developing respect and a cautious attitude can help us save our life and the lives of our loved ones.

Scientists, government officials and business owners should exercise caution so they do not cause irremediable damage to nature's systems and to society. Because of our ignorance about the extensive interconnections of the systems that sustain life on Earth, we should be very cautious and learn to live compatibly with nature's systems in our pursuit of safety, good health and comfort.

Since, every day, we should prepare for what comes next after material life, we show love for our souls when we are cautious about how we seek spiritual knowledge. Moses, Jesus and Muhammad all warned against false teachers and false ideas. Some false information is innocent misunderstanding, but some is deliberate manipulation for personal gain or entertainment.

In the Bible, God promised to send a wonder worker who would teach against the Law. He said this would be a test to see if we really love God completely. (DT 13:1-5) So, we should be aware that false teachers will come – and that this is a test to gauge our commitment to seek God and to be obedient and submissive to God.

100

The Bible cautions us to not make a foreigner (or one with contrary religious beliefs) a ruler over us. (DT 17:14-15) Jesus said false teachers might deceive even the elect – those who elect to seek God. He told us to be careful of wolves in sheep's clothing – those who offer their help in order to gain credibility, but then take control and undermine the mission of a group -- what we would call a change agent. Jesus rejected the interpretations of the Bible popular with the Pharisees, and called them hypocrites. (MT 23:1-29) He also was critical of those who denied the spiritual realm and judgment on the spiritual side of life, such as the businessmen of his day, the Sadducees. Though he taught the good news of God's love for all and the requirement that we love one another, he cautioned us to pay attention and acknowledge how some mislead others to choose selfishness over God.

Since we are judged by the impartial laws of spiritual nature for our thoughts, words and actions, we should be careful about what we believe. Besides thoroughly investigating the source and validity of instructions and teachings, we should ask God in prayer to guide our understanding of information we have received about various religious teachings and social and philosophical ideas that impact our lives. To avoid being led astray, we should be cautious, develop spiritual sensitivity and regularly ask our Creator for guidance before we make decisions. In this way we would show love for our souls, for one another and for God.

Not everyone who becomes a minister, priest, rabbi or imam is seeking God. Some just want an audience, the respect that comes with the job, or political power. However, if citizens become immoral, God blames their priests. (Hosea 4:1-9) It is the priest's responsibility to be involved with the community and teach about God, spirituality and the laws that govern spiritual nature. Isaiah said that bad leaders suited themselves and didn't help the people. (Isaiah 56:10-11) Jeremiah said the shepherds did not search for God, so their flock would be taken from them. (Jeremiah 10:21)

Zephaniah and Malachi pointed out that the priests no longer kept the Law. (Zephaniah 3:4; Malachi 2:7-9) Becoming a minister, priest, rabbi, imam, or other spiritual leader is a spiritual stumbling block for those who are insincere, and for those they lead.

Though God had wanted the Levites to be priests forever and spread teachings about Him to the world, when it became obvious that they had turned inward and rejected their mission, Ezekiel discerned God's communication that He would raise up a descendant of David to shepherd His house. (Jeremiah 12:14-17; Zechariah 2:14-15; Ezekiel 34, 37:20-28) Jesus said that he was that good shepherd. (JN 10:1-8)

We should be cautious with our material sustenance, as well. Being able to store food for long periods of time allowed people to settle in one place and gave them the time and security to turn their minds away from mere survival and towards art, philosophy, science and social issues. It is reported in the Bible that Noah stored a year's worth of food for his family and the animals to eat during the Great Flood. Reminiscent of this practice is the second tithe.

According to the Bible, the first tithe is ten percent of our economic increase. In an agricultural society the gain is in animals, seeds and produce from the land, and ten percent of that increase is supposed to be given to the priests once a year when the harvest is in. In a money based society, salaries are what we gain, and so we give 10% of our (before taxes) money during the course of the year as soon as we receive it.

But there is a second tithe. The second tithe is supposed to be used during the harvest festival each autumn. Since we can't consume all of this ten percent during the one-week festival, it is obvious that the overage is meant to be used during the winter when fewer plants produce a harvest. So, each month during the year we should set aside non-perishable foods such as grains, canned and dehydrated foods as well as spices and teas. By the time of the harvest festival each autumn we should have about a six to nine month's supply of non-perishable foods stocked up. The second tithe gives us a safety net of food for special or unexpected needs. (DT 14:22-26) The Succoth tithe is an exercise in caution that shows love and consideration for ourselves and our families. It also teaches us to think ahead to "what comes next," and encourages us to create that pattern in our decisions and actions.

CAUTION EXPERIMENT

In the Bible we are told that during the seventh year of the seven year cycle (as well as the 50th, or Jubilee, Year) the land should rest. We shouldn't plant or harvest food in those years. We should stock up on non-perishables and avoid buying fresh fruits or vegetables that grow at those times. (LV 25:1-13, 20-22; EX 23:10-11) This is an opportune time to add wild foods to our diets. Some wild foods have more nutritional value than anything you can buy at a grocery store. But you have to be very cautious to identify the correct plants, and to know which parts are edible and how to prepare them. For example, the only part of an elderberry plant that isn't poisonous is the *cooked* berries. The raw berries are still poisonous.

You should prepare ahead of time for the Sabbatical Year by carefully becoming familiar with edible wild plants. I recommend that you buy two or three books about wild foods and cross check the information. Sometimes experts disagree. When that happens, you might want to do more research about that plant.

When looking for wild foods, you should be able to identify every part of the plant – its roots, stem, leaves, flower, fruit and seeds. There are some poisonous lookalikes that vary in only one aspect. (I recommend that you do not harvest wild mushrooms, for this and other reasons.) Even if it is a safe wild plant, it is a good idea to eat only a small amount of it at first to see if your body tolerates it well.

A short beginners list of easy to identify nutritious wild plants would include dandelion leaves and roots, cat tail sprouts, white oak acorns and wild rose flowers and hips. Be sure to wash thoroughly and cook all wild food. It isn't uncommon for wild plants to contain bugs and worms, some of which are too small for you to see.

You shouldn't look for wild food on private property without permission, or in any national or state park, where it is forbidden. When looking for wild food, it is a good idea to wear long sleeves, slacks, heavy boots and disposable gloves. You also may want to wear a veiled bug hat to protect yourself from flying insects. You should avoid going through tall grass or dense shrubs, where there might be venomous snakes or rabid rodents. As an added precaution, you might keep 3 or 4 ounces of salt with you to pack on a wound in the event that you are bitten. The salt will draw out some of the poison while you are on your way to a hospital.

If you add just two or three new wild foods to your skill set every year, you will soon feel more confident when you go hiking or camping in the event that you lose your gear – or get lost yourself. And if you ever have to face an unexpected environmental event that destroys your food supply, you may find it handy to know how to get nourishment from natural sources. Having a background in edible wild foods can lower your panic level in some emergency situations, and it also can help you live a much healthier life day to day.

You may, of course, collect the seeds of your favorite wild plants and cultivate them in your back yard or window garden during years one through six. Remember, though, when collecting wild food or seeds, to always leave at least ten plants, or ten percent of tree fruit, so the plant can regenerate.

FORGIVENESS

As a spiritual law, forgiveness is like a wild card in a card game. It cuts across the laws of karma. It's different.

Though the law, "Pardon your neighbor…and when you pray your sins will be forgiven," appears in the Apocrypha in the Old Testament of the Bible (Ecclesiasticus 28:2 (and see 3-9 TNJB)) this concept is most fully developed in the Christian religion. Jesus emphasized this teaching when he gave the Lord's Prayer. If you forgive others, your heavenly Father will forgive your failings, he said. (MT 6:9-15) Muhammad also said it. If out of love anyone withholds retaliation, it is atonement for himself. (S. 5:45-47)

In Ecclesiasticus (28:1) we are told that, "Whoever exacts vengeance will experience the vengeance of the Lord." In Leviticus (19:18) and Proverbs (20:22) we also are warned against taking revenge. The author of Proverbs said the way of revenge leads to death. Forgiveness is the antidote for this type of spiritual death.

Forgiveness means to give the benefit of the doubt instead of jumping to negative conclusions. It means to not react hatefully to inconveniences and misunderstandings. It is an essential balm for minor careless mistakes, and it helps keep families together and move community services along.

Jesus told his disciples to leave towns where they were rejected and to shake the town's dust from their feet. No cursing, and no revenge. Seeking God's guidance for how to respond to injustice, cruelty and ignorant or careless behavior can help you choose among various techniques for how to move your life forward without getting mired in the muck of revenge.

But forgiveness is not trust. Loving enemies doesn't mean trusting them or condoning evil. We can love others and still hold them accountable for their socially disruptive and personally destructive behavior.

Forgiveness can be instantaneous, but rebuilding trust when trust has been broken is a long process. We shouldn't allow ourselves to be constantly re-victimized. Forgive, yes. But learn from the experience and ask God how to respond to it. We should not trust those who have victimized us -- unless and until they take actions to rebuild the trust that was broken. We should remember the lesson without re-victimizing ourselves. Confucius said to respond to injustice with justice, and to be gentle to those who are kind. (A. 14.36)

There are several laws in the Torah that require kindness and fair treatment to others, including foreigners, but the only laws close to requiring forgiveness of others are those that say to not hate a kinsman and to not take revenge against your neighbor. (LV 19:17-18) It may be that forgiveness of others was cut out of the first five books of the Jewish scriptures – the Torah – though the Day of Reconciliation, when Jews ask God to forgive them, was retained. Everyone wants *to be forgiven.* Not everyone grasps the power of forgiving others. According to the Torah Law, God's forgiveness of your sins is assured if you fast and follow the rituals given in the Bible for the Day of Atonement, also called the Day of Reconciliation.

Jesus reinstated the forgiveness laws that are missing from the Torah. He taught about forgiveness in several different ways. He told a story about a servant who had been forgiven a large debt, but then refused to forgive someone who owed him little. The servant was then held accountable for his whole debt. (MT 18:23-35) Similar to Confucius' teaching to look inward and examine yourself when confronted with someone who is contrary, Jesus said to take the log out of your own eye before you complain about the splinter in another's. (A. 4.17; LK 6:39-42) Two sinners were forgiven. One had a great debt and one had a small debt. Which sinner loved their Master more, Jesus asked. The one who was forgiven more, was the answer. (LK 7:36-47) We should forgive someone who repents 70 times 7, Jesus said. (MT 18:21-22) He told us to love our enemies and pray for those who abuse us. (MT 5:43-48; LK 6:35-36) (Perhaps we should pray that they come to know God.)

Muhammad concurred. Those who avoid wrong doing, and who forgive others, will have a reward with God, he said. Those who are patient and forgiving are truly courageous, and help to resolve conflicts. (S. 42:40, 43) Muhammad said that only Allah can cause your enemies to someday be your friends. (S. 60:7)

Try to imagine what society was like before this powerful teaching and Jesus' example (of forgiving his enemies when he was dying on the cross) drew people to take a leap of faith and experiment with forgiving one another. There was constant tension, extreme clan (and tribe) protectiveness and intense lack of trust. Families and society were always on the verge of exploding from the inner tension of unrelenting fear, hatred and revengeful actions. As the practice of forgiving themselves and one another spread, it opened society up and people could admit to lessons learned, share emotional perspectives, and safely work through many misunderstandings with one another.

The way someone with a Hindu or Buddhist background might say it, is that forgiveness frees us from bad karma that we created both by errors we made in past lives and by the stumbling blocks of law breaking that we have fallen over in our current life. When we decide not to hold grudges or take excessive revenge, we free ourselves from being spiritually bound to those from whom we have experienced trauma in this life or another.

Something happens to us chemically and emotionally when we exercise this power. First, we begin to feel differently. Then we find ways to create gentler treatment towards ourselves and others for errors. This changes our social environment. Other people begin to forgive us for our innocent mistakes because they can see that we are making an extra effort to build a relationship with them and to build the community. The good vibrations spread.

Because we have changed spiritually and chemicaly we think differently, interpret what we see and hear differently, and notice things in our environment that we didn't notice before. As the song says, "There were bells on the hill but I never head them ringing, no I never head them at all, 'til there was you." ('Til There Was You by Meredith Wilson for the 1957 play, "Music Man.") When our feelings change, so do our perceptions and, as a result, our decisions and actions.

The conundrum of forgiveness is that, in spite of forgiving others we must also hold them accountable for serious breaches of the laws that govern spiritual nature -- for their own spiritual health, as well as for family and community stability. Forgiving does not mean condoning evil. Moses, Isaiah and Ezekiel all taught that deliberate law breaking should not be condoned. (Numbers 15:30-31, 33:55-56; Isaiah 1:10-20; Ezekiel 18:5-32) When we condone evil we encourage others in the community to copy that behavior. We also become accomplices, entering into the spiritual rhythm of that error and, therefore, into the inevitable correction that will come to the participants.

Condoning law breaking is not an act of love. It leads the errant party and all who choose immoral behavior because of their un-reprimanded example to greater turning from God. This is an act of cruelty, not love. Those who condone law breaking are afraid the law breaker won't like them if they object to their behavior. They fear the person more than God. But we have to be brave and risk incurring the displeasure of law breakers.

The way to hold someone accountable with love and forgiveness, Jesus taught, is to talk with the person privately and then, if necessary, with counselors. If there is no resolution, bring the matter to the community, or church. If the person continues in their law breaking, Jesus said they should be shunned. (MT 18:15-17) This simple act informs others in the community that there are unpleasant consequences for breaking the Fundamental Laws that govern the spirit, and that the family and community are united in trying to lead the law breaker to repentance for their own and the community's stability. In every generation there are some who become examples of careless or misguided behavior and who, if they are reprimanded, save by example countless others from choosing to copy their actions.

By supporting churches and their outreach programs, we make it obvious to the community that spiritual teaching is available and that all are invited to participate in it. But we shouldn't change the teaching of the church to condone, and thereby encourage, people who break the laws that govern spiritual nature. Nor should we insert ourselves into groups where their members are aware of God and have already rejected those laws. We also should not honor them, as if they are examples all should follow. If we keep them out of select activities, perhaps they will reconsider and repent.

Major breaches of law, of course, should be dealt with at a court of law in order to protect the innocent and the victims. At a court of law, the parties can explain the reasons for their actions. Then the repercussions caused by their actions can be reviewed and a response can be crafted that is in the best spiritual interests of those who were involved and of the community at large.

While God loves every soul endlessly, we are all nevertheless individually, automatically judged according to the laws God created. God doesn't stop loving us when we break a law, but we set ourselves up for the natural repercussions that are built into the cause and effect material and spiritual realms. So, we should try to live by the laws, both to create better order and functionality in this life and to prepare for what comes next after material life.

FORGIVENESS EXPERIMENT

The forgiveness experiment is to keep the Day of Remembrance on the new moon day of the seventh lunar month of the year. (LV 23:23-24) (Count the first month as the new moon closest to the spring equinox, March 21.) During the Day of Remembrance, remember disagreements you have had with others and errors you have made yourself during the previous twelve months. Consider the "log in your own eye" when you evaluate how others have treated you. Ask God for guidance in your relationships, and for how to seek forgiveness and make restitution where needed. Work at forgiving others for the following ten days – in person, by telephone or in writing – throughout your relationships. Put situations that can't be resolved into God's hands, knowing that the laws of spiritual nature will work to correct unresolved issues. Then, on the Day of Atonement, on the tenth day of the seventh (lunar) month, fast and do no work, as the Bible says. (LV 23:26-32) Confess your own errors, resolve how you will make restitution where possible and make changes in your lifestyle. Forgive others from your heart. Then absorb God's forgiveness and love into yourself.

JOY

Ancient societies were replete with holidays and festivals, where governments treated their citizens to feasts and the merry making lasted for days, or weeks. Some ancient societies observed the release of slaves and the remission of debts during holidays, practices that were written into the

Bible as laws to be observed every seventh (sabbatical) years and at the fifty year jubilees.

Ancient festivals marked special times, such as the celebration to bring back the sun at the winter solstice (Saturnalia, for example, and the re-dated celebration of Jesus' birth – both close to December 21) and New Year's day, which originally was celebrated at the spring equinox when plants begin to revive.

The holidays observed by most religions are scheduled using the lunar calendar. The seventh day Sabbath (in Judaism and some Christian sects) is a celebration of the four phases of the moon that make up each lunar month, which the ancients used when planting crops. Christianity alone uses the solar calendar, except for Easter.

Ancient poems and plays came from a long oral tradition where people kept their history alive and achieved a sense of belonging by telling the same stories over and over during festival gatherings. Myths and stories often contain an element of truth – be it historical, psychological, religious or even scientific. By retelling these stories during annual celebrations, they built community identity and loyalty. The stories became part of their culture and gave the people a sense of security in being part of a communal family. Governments around the world continue this tradition to foster national identity and patriotism.

According to documents discovered by archeologists, our current practices of celebrating with parades, lights, decorations, feasts, music and rituals are the same practices that people all over the world have used to observe celebrations for thousands of years.

Every religion has holy days, many of which are celebrated with much merry making. Some celebrations are reminiscent of humanity's agricultural heritage and have endured even though societies have changed radically. The spring planting festival, for instance, lives on in the celebrations of Passover, Easter and the Feast of Weeks.

Around the world there are spring festivals to celebrate the new growth of edible food. In some rural areas there is a spring ramp festival. Ramps are wild onions that grow early in the spring. At the festival there may be contests for the best tasting or most creative ramp dish. Wheat festivals have art contests for items made with wheat stalks. Maple sap starts to flow in late February and continues through March. By the end of March many communities have a maple festival to celebrate the harvest.

County and state fairs are reminders of autumn harvest festivals celebrated from prehistoric times, and written into the Bible as the week long Succoth celebration. Hindus enjoy a four-day harvest festival.

Muhammad said to celebrate the praises of Allah on the appointed days. (S. 2:203) The yearly celebration of Ramadan by Muslims commemorates the times that Muhammad fasted while he lived in a cave. It was while being secluded and fasting that he was inspired to create *The Holy Qur'an*, a book of spiritual revelation through poetry. The date to begin Ramadan is calculated according to the lunar calendar. It lasts a month, during which the faithful do not eat between sunup and sundown each day.

Like the Catholic observance of All Saints Day (Halloween) Chinese Buddhists have a holiday called the Ghost Festival, or Ancestor Day, also in the autumn, where connections between the living and the dead, Earth and Heaven and body and soul are remembered.

Buddhists also celebrate the lunar New Year, the Buddha's birthday and, each month, the four phases of the moon.

Entertainment is like desert after a meal. After a time of toil and pressure, it adds a little sweetness to life. Celebrating also releases good chemicals in our brain that aid our ability to think creatively.

Though some criticize Hindus for treating sex as an entertainment art, Hindus say they merely acknowledge natural human interests and that their teachings about sex are fenced in by teachings that the way to be liberated from the reincarnation cycle is through self-discipline and by controlling sexual appetites. Hindus teach that those who choose pleasure as their purpose in life eventually learn that it is a hollow goal and begin seeking something more meaningful. At some point they discover the nourishment of spiritual food.

In traditional Buddhism monks are advised to train themselves to not desire sex, because it leads to entanglements that could produce conflict and strife. In this way, self-discipline increases one's joy in life.

Jesus said several times that those who love life lose it, but those who lose life for his sake find it. This wasn't to teach against joy, but in favor of choosing self-discipline and God's guidance over our own willfulness. Jesus attended weddings, festivals and banquets, and socialized with his friends.

In the Bible, God commands us to celebrate, to be joyful and to praise and remember the One Who gives us good things, and life itself. Moses said that curses accrue to those who do not serve God joyfully. (DT 28:45-47, 12:11-12) Paul reminded us that God loves a cheerful giver. (2 Corinthians 9:7) Muhammad said that God told Moses to establish regular prayer for celebrating His praise. (S. 20:14)

Psalm 98 says, in part, "Make a joyful noise unto the Lord, all the Earth, make a loud noise and rejoice and sing praise. Sing unto the Lord with the harp... With trumpets and sound of coronet make a joyful noise before the Lord, the King. Let the sea roar and the fullness thereof, the world, and they that dwell therein. Let the floods clap their hands, let the hills be joyful together before the Lord, for he comes to judge the Earth with righteousness.... "

Praising God lifts us up out of despair and self-pity. Loud, joyful praise inspires, guides and goads us when we are desperate and lost, as well as when we are dying quietly in self-satisfaction. Celebrate and praise God before sunrise, before sunset, at night and at the sides of the day, Muhammad urged. (S. 20:130)

The sun shines and the rain falls on everyone. It is a sign of our ultimate love and trust for God when we can serve God joyfully even when we are impoverished and weighed down with hardship. Confucius taught that however coarse the fare, show respect for God's provision. (A. 10.8) Inner peace and happiness can come from good behavior and a sweet spirit even during times of trial. Confucius also said that to love the truth is not as good as enjoying it. (A. 6.18)

African slaves, who had come to the United States from places of primitive spirit worship and brutal tribal wars, found something in the Christian religion that brought light to their souls, and they made up beautiful songs as they went about their work. Many of their songs (such as *There Is A Balm In Gilead, He Never Said A Mumblin' Word* and *Swing Low, Sweet Chariot)* are still sung by Christian congregations of every denomination, and speak to our souls today.

Whatever we experience, be it wealth or poverty, good health or injury or illness, a large, loving family or solitude, we should be humble and keep a sweet spirit. We should have joy in our hearts because we have this opportunity while we are in the material realm to reconnect with our spiritual nature, relearn spiritual strengths and skills and prepare to be reborn as loving and submissive souls with our Creator, Who forever loves each of us. Though we are right to mourn our losses, after we learn the spiritual lessons they

114

teach, we can experience peace, wrapped in the love of God.

We should celebrate because we have someplace to prepare to go, and because the way has been given – the light of the world. Jesus and Muhammad were both called the light of the world. Jesus told the Jews that they were the light of the world and to not hide their light under a bushel. (MT 5:14-16) He reminded them that they had been meant to share the light of God's message with all people. Before the sun there was light, the light of God's wisdom and love lighting up our spiritual void. (GN 1:3-4, 14-18)

God gives blessings in the material realm, but wants us to remember that we are also spiritual entities. (Proverbs 20:27) Holy day rituals align our attention with the spiritual side of life. Participating in rituals that show respect and praise for God helps create a rhythm of obedience inside us. Their symbolism touches a responsive part of our spirit and helps prepare in us an atmosphere for spiritual perception.

When we celebrate God, we shift our attention away from ourselves and to our Creator. This can cause an atmosphere within us that helps us recognize and reconnect with our own spirit. So, we should celebrate and praise the Lord with our family and community, in song and dance, in rituals and stories. Observing Holy Days also shows respect for God by acknowledging the rhythms God created in this solar system.

Every soul longs to return to heaven, where there is endless joy and freedom from fear and want. Our celebrations on Earth are a reminder to us that there is a place of joy, peace and plenty from which we came, and that it is a worthy goal to seek and prepare spiritually to return to that place.

So, let's party! Almost any event out of the ordinary provides an excuse for a party – a birth, baptism, new house, test

115

passed, graduation, new business, marriage, promotion, safe return or commemoration of an historical event – to name just a few. (DT 20:5; EX 14:20-15:21; LK 2:21-24)

JOY EXPERIMENT

Jesus told about a woman who threw a party when she found a coin that had been missing. What opportunities have you been missing to have a party, invite friends and celebrate, praising and thanking God for the good things in life?

Keep God at the center of your celebration with stories, songs and games, and by giving an extra gift to your religious group.

CHAPTER FIVE

RESPECT

Respect is fully integrated into material nature's infinite nest of layers. It is in the instinct of a baby elephant that chases egrets to see them fly, but doesn't injure them. It is in the pattern of animals that kill in order to survive, but don't kill for sport. It is an element of spiritual nature that has been infused into material nature to prevent any one law from overriding all the others. Respect is built into material nature in the force and submission patterns within which materials merely change and have an impact in a different way. Where nature is not forced against its laws by humans, there are automatic limitations beyond the bounds of which actions do not intrude.

We see evidence of respect in the push/pull, force/support -- Confucians would say yin/yang -- tension that provides energy for movement and fences in adjustments when there is change. Disrespect – exceeding all bounds – would allow one force to completely either override or undo another. Respect, which is engineered into the universe's design is, ultimately, what keeps the cosmos in functioning balance. Respect also is critically important to us.

Confucius, the master psychologist, succeeded by expecting morality and praising it, rather than by threatening hell for the immoral. To be fully human, Confucius said, develop five habits: respect, freedom from prejudice, a good work ethic, trustworthiness and generosity. (A. 17.6) Respect the young and old, the rich and poor, the educated and illiterate, friends and enemies. All are to be treated with respect, by not intruding on their rights and by not exceeding the limits of propriety. When the government treats its citizens with respect, its citizens will respect and cooperate with their government, he said. For thousands of years the teaching of respect has been ingrained in Chinese society. It is the foundation of Confucianism and a way of life that has anchored the Chinese people through massive social changes.

Respect drives young children to keep challenging themselves to do what they see older siblings and adults do. They imitate those older than they because they respect them and want their respect in return. The desire for respect and acceptance keeps us following laws when no one is around, and leads us to make sacrifices of time, energy and money to build family and community.

To the Buddha, arguing was disrespectful. One should respect the views of others and not insist on one's own view, he said. He also rejected the caste system of Hinduism, which keeps people at the social strata into which they are born, and the sati tradition, according to which widows were burned to death along with the bodies of their deceased husbands. He allowed that both women and men could be his followers. The Buddha was a beggar, as well as a teacher. He showed respect to everyone, no matter what their station in life.

Jesus also survived from the generosity of those he taught. He was a humble man who showed respect to everyone who sought his wisdom – Jews and Samaritans, Romans and other Gentiles, men and women, the ill and aged and the healthy and young. He sent his followers to teach all people the good news of God's endless love and the way to return to God by developing spiritual sensitivity and choosing God's will over their own.

In *Streetwise: Race, Class and Change in an Urban Community*, Elijah Anderson explains that the deepest desire of juvenile delinquents and life course persistent criminals is respect. The street smart feel disrespected because of their poverty, lack of good paying jobs and discrimination. Their tough behavior and criminal activity are efforts to gain respect from their peers.

We show respect for others by accepting their best efforts to respond to their own challenges. We show respect by not violating another person's rights. No gossip, no false witness, no usury, theft or murder. (LV 19:16, EX 20:16-17; DT 24:14-15, 27:25) Fair courts, fair wages and loyalty to their commitments is how governments show respect to their citizens. Confucius said that one who governs should allow people to pursue what benefits them. Treat all people equally. Don't murder. Don't make contradictory demands, and be fair in giving people entitlements, he said. (A. 20.2)

We show **respect for human life** when we recognize and meet our physical needs, and when we take care to not push the body beyond its limits. The same applies to relationships – be they within our family or between nations. Respect requires **humility**, accepting our own limitations in understanding and abilities and not scorning or deriding the limitations of others.

Showing respect by being courteous and considerate can help to defuse explosive situations, safeguard groups and open a way for dialogue so grievances can be resolved.

"A parasite, one who lives without working, doesn't feel bound by any moral tie to his fellows, but regards them simply as things, instruments meant to serve and amuse him," wrote William Bonger (about capitalists) in, *Criminological Theory Past to Present.* Those who disrespect others create imbalance in the social network, from the nucleus of the family to the functioning of the nation and beyond. This could eventually lead to revolution if the disrespected have no peaceful way to air their grievances and achieve needed change.

It is disrespectful to the young, the ill, the injured and the aged to not **work** to make society function with essential services available to all. There is always much that needs to be done to maintain and improve communities, and it also gives us self-respect when we are engaged in meeting these needs, whether through a paying job or through volunteer work.

Machiavelli held that a leader should terrorize his subjects and secure his rule through fear. Confucius taught that in order to secure his rule, a leader must be moral and show respect for his subjects, earning their respect in return.

When we show respect for others it has an impact on our own body chemistry and, consequently, our health. It is one of the reciprocal powers. Love others as you love your own soul is a powerful, practical truth. As we show respect and love to others we release good chemical reactions inside ourselves and give respect and love to our own body chemistry.

If someone goes so far as to curse someone, he goes beyond just angry words and takes deliberate and revengeful actions that would undermine the person's material security or strength. This negatively alters the condition of the individual's own body and soul. What we do to others comes back to us, not just in karmic events but also in chemical reactions within us.

Part of our spiritual development is linked to the **respect** we show **for the natural environment** that sustains us. When we use unsustainable environmental practices, we show disrespect for the Designer and Creator of this solar system and it diminishes our spiritual sensitivity, strengths and skills.

By way of warning, Jesus told a story about a servant who got drunk and abused other servants. When the servant was evaluated by his master, he was put with those who were "untrustworthy." (LK 12:45-46) When we abuse the Earth – and support businesses that abuse the Earth – we demonstrate that we can't be trusted to behave responsibly toward the planet that sustains us. In a future life we may well come into a land that is distressed, where it is hard to grow food or find security. We will experience what we caused when we acted with disrespect toward the Earth.

Out of self-respect, we **defend ourselves** if we are physically attacked. Every living animal tries to avoid capture and destruction. The designed purpose of every animal is to continue its species and so, instinctively, it strives to survive. Whether we are conscious of it or not, our designed purpose is to learn spiritual lessons, and our spirit would have us cling to life in order to seek out and learn those lessons.

We are able to learn the spiritual lessons we need in order to return to where we were before we came into the realm of time and substance because we have free will. We should not squander the opportunities it allows by using our free will selfishly. When we behave selfishly we close our spiritual sensibilities and miss perceiving information that is critically important to our spiritual future. When we show respect for ourselves, one another and our Creator by choosing to live within the limits of the laws that govern the spiritual and material realms, the resulting positive tension strengthens our spiritual sensibility and we open ourselves up so that our spiritual development may be guided by the Living Power that designed us and gave us free will.

We show respect for the spirit within us when we prepare for our inevitable life after death with as much gusto and diligence as we prepare for a career, and with as much attention and love as we give our families and other passionate interests. We are on Earth only a short time, and we have much to learn to prepare for our longer time in the spiritual realm. We must stay alert and humble and choose carefully in order to prepare for what comes next.

RESPECT FOR HUMAN LIFE

One way we show respect for human life is by maintaining good physical health. The Ayur Veda of India emphasizes a medicine system based on balancing energies. It teaches us about chakras, yoga and massages. It also explains how to use herbs and minerals for good health.

Because ancient Taoists in China sought physical immortality, they experimented with thousands of kinds of plants and their combinations. They wrote an extensive pharmacopeia, a treasure of information that is still largely undiscovered in western countries today. Nevertheless, in countries around the world there are Chinese herb shops that stock hundreds of spices, herbs and teas. It is common for their patrons to request packages of unique blends to give as gifts to honored guests at festive occasions. In their intense investigation of the needs of the human body, Taoists also discovered acupuncture and healing massages and exercises.

The Bible's rules about food are intended to protect our health. We should not eat any animal fat or blood. Modern science has linked animal fat and blood to heart disease and cancer. We should eat a little bit of salt with all grain foods. Salt is necessary for life. It facilitates cell function and is necessary for healthy brain function. (LV 2:13, 17:10-12, 14 and 7:26-27, 3:17) (Other rules are found at Leviticus 11.) The Bible also teaches that, out of respect for others, those with a contagious disease should voluntarily separate themselves from the community until the disease is cured. (NU 5:1-3)

Jesus healed the sick, in part, because his teachings, when accepted by faith, caused changes in the thoughts and feelings of his listeners, and those emotional changes caused changes in their body chemistry. It was the change in their chemistry that resulted in their being healed. Faith healing goes on today, but in order for it to be long lasting those healed must seal the change in their physical chemistry with new behavior habits that reinforce the thoughts and words that initiated the change. (MT 12:43-45) Jesus lamented that people who were set in their ways wouldn't change and be healed. (MT 13:15 (P))

We must respect and protect our physical life, because it is while we are here that we prepare for life in the spiritual realm. In addition to what we eat and drink, everything we think, say and do here has an impact on our physical chemistry, as well as on our soul's condition, which is sealed, for the most part, when we leave the material realm and transition into the spiritual realm.

In the material realm, as part of our interdependent social order, we all develop within soul groups. In our various groups of family and acquaintances we change and grow materially and spiritually. Leaving before the time that is organically natural according to the long term needs for each spirit and its soul group, breaks laws that govern spiritual nature. Death may come by disease, accident or an event of nature, but for someone to commit suicide – whether deliberately or through deliberate carelessness – or to commit premeditated murder (except as punishment for premeditated murder, as decided by a court of law) interferes with the laws of spiritual nature that are working for the edification of the individual and those within the group.

The laws that govern the spiritual realm hold us answerable for our own life -- and for that of our neighbors. Suicide and murder are forbidden. No one should deliberately jeopardize a person's life – their opportunity for spiritual learning and preparation. (GN 9:5; EX 20:13) As a deterrent to premeditated murder, the Bible says that a murderer's life cannot be ransomed; he must die. (NU 35:31, 33-34) According to the rules of karma, he will die, either before finishing his own spiritual mission in this life or in a future life when he is at the same age as was his current victim.

Muhammad said that the murder of a believer draws God's wrath and curse upon the murderer. (S. 4:93) He said that there is a double penalty for killing without just cause. (S. 25:68-69) In the Bible God warns, "The innocent and the righteous you shall not slay, for I will not justify the wicked," and that anyone who murders his neighbor in secret is cursed. (DT 27:24; EX 23:7 (P)) Anyone (such as a judge or a false witness) who takes a bribe, either to help acquit someone who murdered an innocent person, or to cause the death of an innocent person, also is cursed. (DT 27:25)

For one reason or another, some souls may come into this life with either a special spiritual mission or an extra burden of negative karma. Being taken out by accident or disease when they are children may set up the opportunity for constructive changes in their soul group, or help dissolve some of their own negative karma. Everyone comes into life with a cup of experiences to drink. When someone leaves as a child the death itself dissolves some of the painful experiences that were in their cup and they reincarnate with a full measure of good experiences in their next life.

We sometimes meet people who seem to have an easy life. Their opportunities for success abound. It may be that they died early in a previous life and came back with an extra measure of good experiences in this one. This, of course, does not accrue if a person leads himself or herself to an early death by deliberate carelessness or suicide – as this would disrupt the organic development of their spiritual pattern. It would show disrespect for their own soul, as well as that of their soul group.

Providing the opportunity for life in the material realm to other souls, and responding to their interest in the spiritual realm by teaching them how to make choices that help them develop spiritual well-being, is one of the most important missions we can have in life. Teaching children about the laws of spiritual nature and reinforcing the teaching by example, as well as with songs, stories, rituals, celebrations and disciplines, leads them to learn about God and to experience God's presence and guidance.

The Creator of the spiritual and material realms is intimately aware of every soul, and watches over every child. God does not want any child to be mistreated or led astray. Parenting is a sacred trust and childhood is an especially vulnerable time of life. It is the opportune time to plant the seeds for spiritual success that will grow as the child matures. Jesus firmly warned that anyone who causes a child who believes in him to sin would be better off thrown into a sea with a millstone around his neck. (MT 18:6-10) This is not limited to physical abuse and exploitation. Consider the avalanche of immoral laws and misinformation given to the public today. It's sad for our youth, as well as for those who change the laws and deliberately give misinformation to youth! According to the laws of spiritual nature, they will also be held accountable.

Parenting is an important part of the human experience and it teaches many spiritual skills. It is also important if one reincarnates, because it means that those who treat their children well will have a good family experience to come back to.

While life is precious, it is also important to limit our family size in order to keep Earth as a place for other souls to incarnate and learn their spiritual lessons. Because of relative safety, good medical help and readily available nutritious foods, the world's population increased from three billion in 1950 to over seven billion in 2015. Doubling the human population every 50 years will soon drive us all off the planet. Birth control should be taught in all schools, beginning in fourth grade. But there are safe and unsafe methods of birth control. Birth control chemicals are unsafe for humans and significantly disrupt animal life.

Birth control pills and injections use excess estrogen to prevent pregnancy. Excess estrogen lodges in a woman's body fat so that even after she stops using the chemical it can interfere with his development, if she becomes pregnant with a baby boy within a year or two after ceasing to use the chemical. This can result in the baby boy having unnaturally small genitals. Why doesn't the government ban birth control chemicals? Perhaps they consider it a form of population control. It would be more socially stabilizing to make population control a subject taught in schools and kept alive in ad campaigns, and to make safe birth control methods free and easily available. This extra estrogen also ends up in water systems and disrupts fish and animal reproduction in the same way.

Safe methods of birth control should be paid for by our taxes – because it is critically important that population size be controlled in order to continue life on Earth. Humans are the major users and polluters of Earth's resources. We have no natural predators – except other humans. Therefore, we must voluntarily limit our population size so human beings can continue to live within the amount of resources available on Earth.

EXPERIMENT FOR RESPECT FOR HUMAN LIFE

Many years ago, while I was suffering from a debilitating cold, this cure came to me in answer to a prayer. I've been sharing it with others ever since, and you are welcome to share it with others as well. It is a very easy, natural and effective cure for all cold-like viruses – and more.

To immediately stop a cold or flu in its tracks, stop eating grain foods (such as bread, pasta, rice, oatmeal, corn, etc.) milk products, eggs, meat and sugar (even cough drops and fruit juice with sugar) and EAT ONLY ORGANIC FRUITS AND VEGETABLES that have been washed before being peeled, cut or cooked. Use this method just once and you will know how to keep yourself and your family cold and flu free forever!

Try this diet for just one day and you'll see how powerful it is! If your cold or flu is full blown, keep the diet for three complete days (start at supper before the first day and continue until breakfast on the fourth day) and the virus won't come back. Don't overdo the diet. If symptoms persist on day four, wait and see if your immune system responds.

Be sure to read ingredients labels – some canned fruits contain sugar or corn syrup. Even canned peas may contain sugar. Remember, corn is a grain, not a vegetable. Since the skins of produce may have been dipped in wax or chemicals, it is best to peel what you eat raw. Powdered foods and spices may contain fillers not listed on their label, and should be avoided. Don't eat nuts, stevia or honey or drink coffee or tea during the diet.

Salt is essential for cell function. You should add a little salt to the vegetables. Garlic is also a healthful additive. Garlic is antiseptic, antifungal, antibiotic, a chelating agent (it removes heavy metals from the body) and it is loaded with vitamins and minerals.

You can use garlic in a four bean soup. Use dry or canned beans such as chick peas, kidney beans, pinto beans and lima beans cooked with garlic cloves cut up, and fresh parsley leaves. Add lemon juice and salt to your taste.

Parsley is another health staple. It is loaded with vitamins. It also makes a nice tea. Boil three cups of filtered water for 10 minutes, take if off the stove and add two tablespoons of fresh or dried parsley. Cover and steep for 10 minutes, then strain, if you like, and add a pinch of salt.

Be sure the fruit and vegetables you eat are certified organic. Some studies have shown that genetically modified foods weaken the immune system, among other things. Non-GMO is not the same thing as organic. The food may have been modified by a different process, grown with biosolid fertilizer or protected with harsh pesticides.

Be sure to boil even spring water five to ten minutes before using it. If you must use tap water, filter it or let it settle in a glass container 24 hours, then pour off the top half and boil that for ten minutes before using it. If your boiled spring water shows residue in the bottom of the pan and/or oil on top of the water, perhaps you should change brands.

Even if you aren't sick, you can feel the power of this diet if you use it for one 24 hour day. As a three-day diet it can be beneficial for some other infections as well as cold and flu. But be strict! Don't take one bite of food off this diet for the full one or three-day period.

If you take medication, have had a transplant or are pregnant you should check with your doctor before using any diet.

After a cure it is customary to say a prayer of thanks to God and make a special donation to your religious organization.

RESPECT FOR THE NATURAL ENVIRONMENT

Hinduism teaches that the Earth is a training ground for the spirit, a place where we learn spiritual discipline and sensitivity and where we are able to prepare for eventual liberation from the reincarnation cycle. We should protect the Earth so it is always available to souls that need it.

Ahimsa, the Hindu concept to not harm by thought, word or deed, is the first of Hinduisms Five Moral Restraints and is the reason why many Hindus are vegetarian. Likewise, Buddhists teach that we should not harm any living thing. The goal of ancient Taoism also was to live in unity with nature. In order to not harm by thought, word or deed we must live sustainably as part of the natural environment.

By living sustainably, we show respect by preserving Earth so future souls (and even our own, if we need to reincarnate) have the opportunity to come to Earth and learn the spiritual lessons that can be learned here. It also shows respect for our own souls if we are not in debt to the material realm when we leave it.

Today, we have enough knowledge to force our will on some of the natural environment – to exceed its organically developed limits, to intrude and disrupt its order, to interfere with the life protecting design engineered into Earth -- and create chaos.

The way we lost our spiritual powers originally was by acting against the laws of our spiritual nature. Today we are doing the same thing with material nature, and jeopardizing Earth. One of the spiritual lessons we must learn is how to have power and not abuse it.

We show disrespect for Earth by creating civilization-destroying nuclear weapons. Besides toxic nuclear waste, the threatened use of nuclear weapons poses a risk to the whole planet. Their detonation by accident or design could, at the very least, cause a nuclear winter that would destroy our food supply. One reason the United States keeps creating and stockpiling nuclear bombs is because its economy is tied to weapons manufacturing. An excessively large percent of the U.S. gross domestic product is generated by the defense industry.

As a by-product of a usury based economy, when manufactured products saturate their country of origin, business owners seek materials and customers in other countries. History shows that wars have been used to achieve business goals. Therefore, it is clear that in order to live compatibly with other nations and sustainably on Earth we must create a sustainable economic model. This would end the need for the manufacture of nuclear weapons and make the Earth a safer place for us all.

We create chaos with the form of capitalism that allows infinite stock dividends for which no work is done, as well as compound interest -- a form of legalized theft. Usury based capitalism requires planned obsolescence -- the practice by which business owners create products to be weak so the products must be continually rebought. This shows disrespect for the Earth by draining the Earth of natural resources, by engineering synthetic products that do not biodegrade, and by dumping enormous amounts of toxic waste into the Earth – too much to be absorbed and safely processed.

Plastics and other pollutants are killing the oceans – the source of half of Earth's oxygen and the base of our food chain and life on Earth. Single use plastics such as grocery bags, drink bottles, bottles for detergents, shampoos and other items, covers on disposable diapers, some toys and even cheap writing pens and plastic razors take *centuries* to break down, and never completely biodegrade. When they are burned or broken up they become micro plastics that seep into our water and food supply and disrupt our immune and endocrine systems and genes.

While degradable plastics are being experimented with, it is not yet known what is the long-term effect on the human body of food that is stored or served in those new style plastic containers. Just as with current plastics, it will take decades to learn their long-term effects on ourselves and the environment.

We have created something that is easy and cheap to make, usable in a multitude of ways and being manufactured day and night, **but we can't get rid of it!** Scientists estimate that at the current rate of manufacturing and disposal the oceans will be so overloaded with plastics that they will die before the end of this century. Synthetic creations don't naturally evolve, and they don't naturally dissolve – so we are stuck with them, in one form or another, for centuries. They circumvent nature, showing disrespect for God's creation. Since they are not natural, they do unnatural things to the environment and to our bodies.

Pushing dangerous products and procedures on the planet in order to "thrive" economically threatens everyone's physical survival. When thriving economically is the primary goal, scientists, business owners and government officials fail to look for and take into account the expanded impact of their decisions.

Microbiologists tell us that all life is connected from its earliest forms. When we interrupt the organic development of life by cloning, genetic engineering, taking good bacteria out of milk, fracking or adding synthetic non-biodegradable substances to foods and to the environment, we challenge plants and animals to adjust out of the context of their organic development to these sudden and unnatural changes. Our body chemistry also struggles to adjust when it is loaded with unnatural elements. These practices rob us of what would be natural aids to our immune and nerve systems. They disrupt our physical and mental health by disrespecting the organic development of life forms.

The reasons pests and bacteria evolve resistance to pesticides and synthetic antibiotics, respectively, is that those man-made chemicals don't have the whole range of balancing micro-chemicals that develop in nature organically. Scientists find a quick, financially lucrative solution that works, but they cannot replicate with chemicals the complex, long-term solutions the environment creates organically. So they increase and expand their damage by making ever more powerful pesticides and antibiotics, rather than taking a step back and using natural techniques.

After all, over thousands of years, pests and bacteria have not evolved resistance to natural pest control tactics (such as burning off the field at the end of the growing season, spacing plants wide apart, keeping the field clean of debris, using border plants that attract helpful insects and letting the land rest every seven days and seventh year) or natural medicines (such as the super antibiotic – garlic). Epidemics in the past have been traced to dietary deficiencies and unsanitary conditions.

Some scientists have said that genetically modified foods weaken the human immune system and make us susceptible to diseases we previously were able to ward off. Foods are genetically modified to serve financial goals, ignoring their impact on the population and the planet.

Further, by bioengineering some pests to become extinct, scientists take a critical link out of nature that they don't understand the expanded impact of, and that they can never replace! This could cause a cascade of unexpected problems for which there is no solution -- since the link has been extinguished.

To be holy means to separate ourselves from the world for God. (LV 19:2) While we are on mission to do God's work in the world, we should practice an attitude of detachment so that we do not become obsessed with money or material pleasures. Jesus advised us to seek a spiritual goal and to not be overly worried about our material needs. (MT 6:24-34) Competition may be useful to enhance life, but unregulated and loosely regulated competition becomes a tool with which to cheat the poor, destroy the environment and devalue life.

Confucius was opposed to competition (except in archery). (A. 3.7) The Buddha was opposed to the attitude of possessiveness, and of private ownership of things. Private ownership leads to covetousness, competition and conflict, he said. He advised his followers to train themselves to seek liberation from the avarice in the world by denying their desire for material things.

Something that lifts us out of our animal nature to develop as human beings is self-limiting our desires and behavior.

Even if we have the knowledge and opportunity to do something, we may choose to exercise restraint because of long term negative consequences of acting on that knowledge. Birth control chemicals, nuclear weapons, biological weapons, cloning, nanoparticles, fracking, genetically modified organisms and synthetics all attack Earth's natural life-sustaining balance. They are all the result of choosing financial gain at the expense of nature's infinitely complex interconnected nest of systems. We have the knowledge and power to do these things, but they all interfere with the delicate, ultimately life protecting, balance of nature. To be mature in our humanity we must show respect for one another by creating a sustainable economic system, and show respect for Earth by not forcing its systems beyond their organically developed bounds.

To begin with, we show respect for nature's rhythms by living by the sustainable plant, animal and land use traditions and observances that we already have. Though agriculture is practiced all over the world, not all religions offer guidance for plant, animal and land management. The Bible gives several techniques.

The Bible's guidance includes the weekly Sabbath rest for the land, as well as 7th and 50th year rests for the land, keeping plants and animals genetically pure, not castrating male animals, not eating the fruit of trees until the 4th year, not killing a mother animal and her young on the same day and not killing a young animal until its 8th day (after its blood has developed vitamin K) not sowing with mixed seed, not destroying fruit trees, not plowing with two different kinds of animals together, not muzzling an animal that is treading grain, and many other laws. The Bible is a farmer's sustainability guide book. We only have to follow it. (LV 26:33-35, 25:1-12, 22:27-28; DT 22:9-10, 20:19-20, 25:4)

Muhammad told us to not waste by excess. God doesn't love those who waste, he said. (S. 7:31) When we put aside our pride and greed to live sustainably with nature we live a simpler life. Then, as we become more sensitive to Earth's natural rhythms, we also become more sensitive to our own spiritual nature and are better able to perceive its patterns. Living sustainably and with respect for the world around us helps us reach our spiritual goals of personal and social balance.

Jesus warned that those not trustworthy with money won't receive what is their very own -- that is, the reinstatement of spiritual skills and strengths that have eternal value. (LK 16:10-13) This warning applies to our relationship with Earth's resources as well. If we can't be trusted to be responsible stewards of Earth, then we can't be trusted to responsibly use spiritual strengths with which to transcend the cycle of serial lives. We diminish ourselves spiritually when we miss the opportunity that living sustainably affords to demonstrate to our own soul as well as to the Designer and Creator of both realms that we can be trusted with having power and not using it for selfish, and ultimately self-destructive, ends.

Many economists are concerned about the suicidal nature of usury based capitalism. Some suggest solutions. Dr. Herman Daly has many ideas for a "steady state" economy and shares them in his website and books. Economists at the World Economic Association publish books and a journal with analyses and suggestions. Journals from the Post Autistic Economics group provide insight and direction. Books by Fritjof Capra and Gunter Pauli (such as: *Steering Business Toward Sustainability*) Tim Jackson (*Prosperity Without Growth: Economics for a Finite Planet*) David C. Korten (*Agenda For A New Economy, From Phantom Wealth to Real Wealth*) and Lester R. Brown (*Eco-Economy, Building An Economy For The Earth*) are among those that also address this issue.

After we create a sustainable economic model, we will be in a better position to find ways to live sustainably with nature. Then scientists can turn their talents to how to reverse-engineer synthetic products so it is possible to safely dispose of all their macro and micro parts.

It is not in our spiritual self-interest to wait for the government to legislate sustainability. We must assume personal responsibility. When we are evaluated at the end of our lives, it is our personal decisions and actions for which we will be held accountable.

EXPERIMENT FOR RESPECT FOR THE NATURAL ENVIRONMENT

Following are a few techniques for living sustainably. If by way of experiment you add one item or habit a month, by the end of a year you will have experienced greater sensitivity and increased your respect for your own, and Earth's, natural rhythms.

Sustainability is a game of cooperation where we are challenged to live compatibly within nature's community of life. In nature, plants and animals create living networks and systems that generate no waste. One species' waste becomes another species' food. For us to live sustainably we must learn nature's networks and systems and devise ways to live in sync with them.

We can begin at the beginning. The foundation of life on Earth is in the health of the lowly phytoplankton. Phytoplankton are tiny plants found in the oceans. They are the base of our food chain. Phytoplankton are food for most forms of fish life, and fish are food for birds and mammals. In addition, phytoplankton produce more than half of Earth's oxygen. Changes in the health, amount and distribution of phytoplankton impact the entire food chain, all the way up to humans. You can see why protecting phytoplankton is critically important to sustaining life on Earth.

When phytoplankton growth is artificially accelerated by sewage discharge, agriculture fertilizers and animal waste runoff, it blocks sunlight from ocean areas that incubate many species of fish. This decreases the amount of bait fish available for larger fish to eat. Then, when the excessive amount of phytoplankton dies, their decomposition sucks oxygen out of the water, causing more fish death.

One way we disrupt the ecosystem of the all-important phytoplankton is by pouring excessive waste in rivers, which run into oceans. Some of this is human waste. There are products on the market that can be used to mitigate this onslaught of waste. One is the electric, waterless Incinolet toilet, a home use toilet that incinerates waste rather than discharging it into a sewer. Another is a toilet that was created for boats and cabins: the AirHead, marine class MSD type III toilet, which is waterless and non-electric. It would be an easy thing for people who own their own home or business to install a waterless toilet.

The way environmental scientists have been responding to this crisis is to turn sewage sludge into biosolid fertilizer used to grow food. The problem with this approach is that in developed countries our sewage sludge is loaded with toxic chemicals from pharmaceuticals, manufacturing, cleansers, cosmetics and other sources. When these chemicals are drawn up into plants fertilized with biosolids they come into our food chain and cause illnesses. Some poisons accumulate in the body and are not safe even in small amounts. Waterless toilets keep human waste out of waterways and oceans, and out of biosolid based agriculture fertilizers. We can have a powerful impact on the foundation that supports life on Earth by simply taking responsibility for our own waste.

Waste from cattle and poultry raised on corporate farms also ends up in water ways and threatens phytoplankton. Every aspect of farming is healthier when farms are small, diverse and balanced. In a diverse farm, the waste from livestock is dried for a year and then used as fertilizer.

To reduce the amount of animal waste that goes to the ocean, some people choose to be vegetarian, or to at least eat a meat-free diet one or two days every week. In her book, *Diet For a Small Planet,* Frances Moore Lappé points out that meals that combine a carbohydrate, a dairy product and a legume (beans, peas, lentils or peanuts) or an egg provide as much protein as meat. This particular high protein combination is also better for your brain. She gives recipes, as well as background research, in her book.

The land to meat ratio of raising animals for food is so great that, rather than use high yield genetically modified seed to "feed the world," we might rethink how much meat we eat. It is estimated that it takes sixteen pounds of grain to produce one pound of beef. The land used to grow food for hogs and cattle could be used to grow food that would go much further to feed people. The price of meat would go up, encouraging people to eat less of it. Also, if state laws did not prohibit the sale of wild caught deer and other ruminants (while the state regulates their numbers) we would not need bears and wolves to keep their populations in balance, and we would reinstate a valuable source of meat that doesn't require farmland to provide its food.

Besides the onslaught of animal waste coming from corporate farms, on large monoculture farms fruits and vegetables are especially vulnerable to disease and pests, making it necessary to use toxic pesticides to protect them. Besides impairing human health, and weakening the immune systems of critically important bees and bats, these poisons also end up in rivers and oceans where they cause massive fish death. Fruits and vegetables stay healthier on small, diverse farms. Recent studies show that small, sustainable, organic farms even enjoy a greater profit margin than corporate farms.

Corporate farms are protected by subsidies and tax loopholes. One way to support diverse, small farms is both through appropriate government legislation to change tax and subsidy laws, and through Community Supported Agriculture (CSAs).

In the 1970's, Professor Booker T. Whatley's landmark 25 acre farm earned $100,000 a year. One of the five essential criteria for small farms to thrive, he said, is to sell memberships in the farm in exchange for whatever the farm produces. This is the concept behind CSAs. In CSAs, members support a local farm by paying a yearly fee. For this they receive a portion of the farm's products. You can research CSA farms in your area through Local Harvest.org or by calling your local agriculture department.

Some farms allow their CSA members to help with planting, weeding and harvesting on weekends of their choice. This makes a great family outing. Children who participate in gardening are much more likely to eat vegetables they have helped plant and watched grow. Studies have shown that children who participate in gardening when they are young are more likely to grow up feeling a bond with nature that translates into choosing a sustainable lifestyle when they are adults.

Capitalists are at war with the tender phytoplankton. In the system of capitalism money is more important than the impact the means to make money has on the environment and the long-term effects on their own and their community's health. In their frenzied pursuit of money, they pour many chemicals into the environment that end up in the oceans and that are taken up by shellfish, seaweed and fish both large and small.

Capitalists add hormones to animal feed to make livestock grow bigger, faster and produce more (meat, milk or eggs). These hormones are passed along to us and cause us to crave more food, too. Then they pass through us and into the environment and continue their unnatural effect. For dairy cows, growth hormones cause more milk than the market can absorb. Rather than discontinuing the growth hormones, corporate farmers take good bacteria out of milk to extend its shelf life. This causes a chemical imbalance in our bodies, because we need that good bacteria. In addition, cows that are given growth hormones have a shorter life span than others. Besides affecting humans, all these unhealthy changes eventually spread throughout the environment and into the oceans, upsetting the ecosystem of animals and fish life alike.

To compete in the sale of foods, capitalists add artificial flavors and colors to foods. These artificial additives have an impact on the human nervous system and brain. Nanoparticles are used to enhance food appearance and flavor and to enhance cosmetics, cleansers and other things. The long term effects on humans and the environment of synthetic nanoparticles has not been assessed, but it has been noted that those who work with nanoparticles have a higher incidence of lung cancer. It's possible that, like asbestos, synthetic nanoparticles can accumulate in the body and lead to health problems. It has also been shown in studies that metal nanoparticles have shown up in sewage sludge, and hence in biosolids used to grow food, as well as in storm runoff that pollutes rivers and oceans. Everything is connected. Nothing on Earth lives in a vacuum.

To make cloth wrinkle free, flame retardant or unbreathable (to hold in body warmth) and to make some kinds of paints, varnishes, lubricants, cleansers, and other chemical compounds sold at stores, those for whom money is more important than the impact they have on their own and their neighbors' health mix up many chemicals that have not been in long term tests that show their impact on humans or the environment. Thousands of chemicals are being used that have not received the full range of long term and unbiased tests to prove all of their repercussions for humans or the Earth. After being on the market for decades, a few of these get better tests if enough customers complain long enough about the health problems that they cause. Meanwhile, these chemicals are poured into and leach into waterways spilling into the oceans, where they disrupt fish life and, hence, the whole chain of life.

There are natural, sustainable alternatives to most of these synthetic enhanced products. There are foods free of artificial additives. There are natural fabrics, paints and cleansers, glass and tin containers (instead of plastics) and many other products. You may have to look for them or ask for them or even order them by mail, but it's worth the extra effort in order to add another dimension to living sustainably.

To live sustainably, products should be designed in such a way that the waste generated from their manufacture can be used as resources cycling through the system. This concept is explained in *Cradle to Cradle*, by William McDonough and Michael Braungert. The Cradle to Cradle Products Innovation Institute certifies businesses that are designed sustainably. Cradle to cradle products are listed at their web site. As part of your experiment, why not look through their list and switch to sustainably made products for those items you wish to buy?

Just as God isn't making any more Earth, God isn't making any more water. We should keep what we have clean and, as populations continue to explode, learn to conserve it. It's easy to replace shower heads with water savers and faucets with aerators so we waste less. We also should wash only full loads of clothes (or dishes) and use water and energy saver appliances. If you live in a house, in the morning before you leave for work you could write down the numbers on your water meter. When you return in the evening check the numbers to see if they are the same. If they aren't, then you have a leak somewhere and you'll save water and money if you find and repair it. You can collect in a barrel rain runoff to water your garden, and mulch around your plants to conserve water.

I am in awe of the many miraculous medicines that are available today. Truly, there are some physical illnesses that respond only to those meds. Nevertheless, there is a tidal wave of unnecessary medicines that are major pollutants and that make their way into drinking water, rivers and oceans. It is widely known that some chronic illnesses can be alleviated with a simple change in diet. Employing just a few methods (see the *Loyalty* and *Respect for Human Life* experiments) with a little self-discipline and dietary control we can all live better, keep a vast amount of toxic chemicals out of our municipal water systems, rivers and oceans, and lessen the impact of synthetic chemicals on animal life and fish life.

To live compatibly with nature, all our chemical product wastes should be recyclable and biodegradable. Currently, there are millions of pounds of plastics and other non-biodegradables floating around in the oceans and threatening the humble phytoplankton as well as all manner of fish. Society's response is to develop landfills, which contain many products that take centuries to biodegrade and which leach toxins into the soil that, besides affecting farmland and drinking water, eventually end up washed into rivers that carry them to the oceans.

The plastic on disposable diapers takes centuries to biodegrade. It is a simple decision whether to live sustainably using either reusable cloth diapers or paper diapers and a reusable plastic cover, or to clog up landfills with plastic. When traveling, gDiapers, which have a lightweight, flushable liner inside a cotton cover, are better than the kind of disposables that end up in landfills. Department stores could show their Green by selling cloth diapers and reusable plastic covers at cost. Their profit would be in enhanced customer relations and a cleaner, more sustainable environment for everyone.

To avoid putting tampons into waste water or landfills women can choose to use a reusable menstrual cup or reusable cotton sanitary pads.

Some detergents, shampoos and cleansers are made in powder or bar form and packaged in paper. Shampoo can also be replaced with some brands of bar soap. Castile, glycerin and some organic soaps tend to be environmentally friendly and safer to use. Laundry detergent can be replaced with vinegar, which is cleaner for the environment. To remove oil stains on clothes, wet the area and rub cornstarch into the stain before washing. Toothpaste can be replaced with tooth powder made of one part salt and four parts baking soda. (The baking soda should feel silky, not grainy.) Any product that includes synthetic fragrance could be dangerous to your health, as well as to the environment. Fragrance chemicals are trade secrets and do not have to pass stringent government review.

Before drinks were marketed in plastic and tin they were in recyclable glass bottles. It would create another industry to return to glass bottles picked up and returned to the manufacturer by a small business in each city. We could also return bottles to stores and receive a credit, and they could be picked up from the stores. Alternatively, at home, if you must have a carbonated drink, you could use a machine that makes it instead of buying it bottled. Reusable packing and shipping boxes could be added to this service. We can easily make this change – and we should.

Here is a sustainable practice. Take your own beverage container when you go to a fast food restaurant and let them fill it with your beverage. When you are finished, dry it with a paper napkin and carry it home to wash. Why put all that unnecessary plastic or wax coated waste into landfills? This could be expanded to include cutlery, straws, and containers that carry fast foods. When going to the grocery store, buy meat wrapped in paper or take reusable containers for meat and vegetables.

Congress should pass a law that makes it illegal to manufacture, transport or use single use plastics. Before there was plastic, hospitals boiled items to sterilize them. They also used UV light. Plastics are killing us, and our leaders need to address this crisis and end the onslaught. A law could give manufacturers and businesses four months to get rid of their single use plastics, and give the government time to teach citizens through an advertising campaign how to adjust. In just four months we could be living in a safer world. Some countries have already made single use plastics illegal.

To be sustainable, however, scientists need to devise ways to live without synthetics altogether. To create them is a power they have, but to live without them is a better use of intelligence and power.

The intent of Freecycle, started by Devon Beal in 2002, is to keep usable products out of landfills. Freecycle manages an international Internet program that facilitates the exchange of products -- for free -- from those who have something to dispose of to those in need of that product. It has over 9 million members worldwide. In some cities, governments have copied the Freecycle style to transfer still usable computers, furniture and other materials between schools, non-profits and government offices. If your city doesn't do this, you could suggest that your city government start this program.

iFixit is a company that sells tools, parts and instructions for how to fix tech toys and keep them out of landfills. If you aren't mechanically minded, they'll provide contact information for an iFixit business in your area.

Thrift stores and consignment stores also help recycle reusable items. Some provide a pick-up service and a tax credit receipt. Thrift stores run by churches often are staffed by volunteers and are not required to pay for rent or utilities.

As a result, their prices are very reasonable. A hundred dollars spent at a thrift store can buy a thousand dollars' worth of clothes, toys, kitchen supplies, furniture, books and other items, and keep many pounds of discards out of landfills. Re-gifting, by giving away what you have received as a gift that you won't use, is another sustainability practice.

If you own a cat, a simple contribution you could make to sustainability is to use the CitiKitty method to teach your cat to use a toilet instead of kitty litter. This has the added advantage of reducing odor and mess in your home, and saving you a few dollars every week on kitty litter.

Another method some cities have developed to keep waste out of landfills is a pay-as-you-throw charge. First, citizens are educated to the various methods for sustainable buying, recycling and composting. Then they are charged by weight for the amount of waste they send to landfills. If your city doesn't do this, you could petition for it.

With a simple law the government could require manufacturers to accept back those of its products that have worn out or ceased working and that would otherwise be sent to a landfill. The manufacturer would be responsible for recycling the products' parts and could offer renovated products at a reduced cost. This would keep an enormous amount of waste out of landfills. If, in addition, manufacturers are required to pay-as-you-throw, it is likely that they will make products that last longer in order to reduce their landfill fee. As part of your sustainability experiment you might lobby the government to pass this legislation. As with recyclable glass bottles and boxes, transporting the used products would create jobs.

The way we create and use energy has a powerful impact on nature's systems. Because of its deadly waste, as well as its potential for catastrophic environmental disasters, nuclear energy is not sustainable. No material thing is 100%

secure. Nuclear reactor waste dumps and stockpiles are tragedies waiting for a trigger.

Coal, oil, gas and even hydroelectric dams already interfere with nature's systems and create ecological imbalances. All fossil fuels use Earth's non-renewable fuel assets and impact climate change. Solar and wind energy systems use perpetually renewable energy and blend into the environment without disrupting it. These systems can produce a limitless amount of clean electricity that can be used in homes, businesses and transportation products.

In order for electric companies to not fight the switch to renewable energy, the government should subsidize their downsizing and help workers obtain training and new employment. To switch your electric company and support renewable energy providers in your state, inquire about them at your state's environmental department.

Electric cars use half the amount of fossil fuel that gas driven cars use, even if the electricity is created by a coal burning plant. There are over a dozen types of electric and hybrid cars on the market. Public transit further saves energy and improves air quality. A bus that transports hundreds of passengers a day keeps hundreds of cars and their toxic exhaust out of use each day.

Our living and work spaces also should be sustainable. Not only the materials used in building them, but also their design and size should be compatible with nature. "Tiny Homes" and homes with multipurpose rooms are becoming popular, not just to save money but also to live more sustainably. Zero Energy Homes are homes that, through advanced design, building products and systems, produce as much energy as they use during a year. When you have a house built or renovated, why not hire a contractor who shares your vision for sustainable living? Information can be found at zeroenergyproject.org. The U.S. Green Building

Council offers Leadership in Energy and Environmental Design (LEED) certification for sustainably built businesses.

Nature sustains life by creating networks that are resilient to change, within limits. To live sustainably we must create networks of knowledge and cooperation, and we must learn how to be resilient too. Rather than indulging in the latest high tech products, we should limit ourselves to use only those that are made sustainably. This would include not buying from computer companies that do not support older models of software, and it would include not supporting companies that deliberately make products to break or wear out quickly.

If we do these simple things: switch to waterless toilets, support diverse, local farms, make single use plastics illegal – or obsolete, by not using them -- recycle usable products, require manufacturers to take back used products and pay-as-you-throw their wastes, educate citizens about recycling and composting and then charge pay-as-you-throw for landfill trash, double insulate our homes, use renewable energy providers and products, electric cars and public transit, switch to fee based, compound-interest-free banking, use barter, countertrade and crowd funding (see the experiment for *Repentance*) invest ourselves in time banks, and petition the government to make safe (hormone free) birth control free we can help change the unsustainable trajectory of usury based capitalism and create a system that protects human life on Earth – and that also protects the foundation of life, the humble phytoplankton.

Books of interest:
50 Simple Things You Can Do To Save Earth, edited by John, Sophie and Jesse Javna
An Inconvenient Truth, by Al Gore
Deep Ecology for the Twenty First Century, edited by George Session
Diet For A Small Planet, by Frances Moore Lappé
Easy Green Living: The Ultimate Guide to Simple, Eco-

Friendly Choices for You and Your Home, by Renee Loux
For the Common Good: Redirecting the Economy Toward Community, the Environment and a Sustainable Future, by Herman Daly, PhD and John B. Cobb, Jr., PhD
Eco-Economy, Building an Economy for the Earth, by Lester R. Brown
FoxFire, (a series of books about sustainable early American crafts and skills) edited by Eliot Wigginton
Our Stolen Future, by Theo Colborn, Dianne Dumanoski and John Peterson Myers
Plan B..., (a series of books) by Lester R. Brown (founder of World Watch Institute; see that website for his books written from 1963-2015.)
Plastic: A Toxic Love Story, by Susan Freinkel

HUMILITY

Of the 42 Divine Principles in the ancient *Egyptian Book of the Dead,* three affirm that the petitioner has not acted insolently, spoken arrogantly or been puffed up with pride. (35, 37, 41)

Humility is an important component of Confucius' teachings as well. A noble person eschews acting with arrogance, crude speech and pointless talk, as well as acting without forethought, he said. (A. 13.3) If one has humility one does no harm but seeks what is best for the whole self, the whole family, the whole community, Earth and the universe. You shouldn't be concerned if someone doesn't recognize your talents; be concerned if you don't recognize theirs, he said. (A. 1.16) Confucius said, if you are a prince and you are wrong but no one contradicts you, this is a practice that will ruin a country. (A. 13.15)

This last piece of advice is a warning for all time that anyone who works to cause laws that prevent honest criticism, is preparing for the ruin of his own soul as well as his community. If no one is allowed to criticize you, by law, then you have a free field in which to break all the laws of spiritual nature and create chaos in society and yourself. Calling honest dissent, respectful criticism or religious dialogue hate speech, and passing laws to make it unlawful for anyone to speak out about an educative issue that someone else chooses to be offended by, stunts our opportunities to learn and grow and creates a pattern that will eventually ruin a country.

Muhammad said that we transgress all bounds when we think we are self-sufficient. (S. 96:6-7) He said that there is no one in Heaven or on Earth but must be God's servant. (S. 19:93) Whatever makes us feel pride tempts us to prefer the material realm over the spiritual realm and draws us away from the rhythm of humility that opens up our spirit to discern God's guidance. No one enters heaven unless they have a servant's heart.

Modesty in dress is an aspect of humility. We should not parade our muscles or our sexual parts in public. Muhammad reminded us to cover up, and don't walk on the Earth with insolence. (S. 7:26, 17:37, 57:23) The Bible teaches this, too. Priests are told to wear breaches. "Adam and Eve" covered themselves with fig leaves. (EX 28:42-43, 20:26; GN 3:7) We are responsible for our example to others, and we should not try to lure others to think constantly about sexual pleasures.

Humility is the foundation of Buddhism. Monks are expected to beg for their daily food, eat only two meals a day, sleep on a bed that isn't raised off the floor and own just what they wear. All of this is so they can master pride, conceit and selfishness – attitudes that lead to sinful thoughts, words and actions.

Jesus said that no one enters heaven without being as humble as a little child. (MT 18:1-4) It is because of their humility that little children are always eager to learn, and feel no anger at being corrected. Adults should try to cultivate these attributes. They would help us throughout life, as well as help us prepare for life in the spiritual realm.

Jesus also was an example of humility. When told that a stranger was casting out devils in his name, Jesus said to leave him alone. (MK 9:38-40) When thrown out of a village, he left without cursing. (LK 9:51-56) He told his disciples that one sows and another reaps. Both are servants of God, and neither should feel pride or jealousy. (JN 4:37-38) Jesus washed the feet of his disciples, and taught that we should be servants to one another and to God. (JN 13:3-17) Jesus often taught servitude. He said that whoever wishes to be first among you, should be a servant to all. He said that our goal should always be to be responsible and worthy servants of God. He told us to be good servants who do not expect anything extra for doing what we are expected by God to do. (MT 24:45-47; MK 10:44; LK 17:7-10, 12:35-48)

Jesus humbled himself and showed respect for women by talking with them, touching them, healing them and teaching them. This broke with the practices of his time where, apparently out of insecurity for their masculinity, men refused to speak even with their wives.

Developing respect for what is servile in human nature, as well as what is assertive, helps sensitize us to the whole nature of the Omnipotent Judge and Creator, Who is also the Omniscient Comforter and Wise Counselor.

Jesus pointed out that that which is highly esteemed among men is an abomination in God's sight. (LK 16:15) He said that those who seek their own glory cannot understand his words. (JN 7:16-18) His parable of the sower (where the Word of God was scattered like seeds and some fell on rocks) showed that the cares of the world can distract and choke our perceptions. Then the word of God becomes ineffective for us. (MT 13:4-23) Spiritual sensitivity is increased when we declutter our emotions from selfish

149

thoughts, and shift our focus away from gaining power, accolades and money. Then we are free to absorb the intentions and hidden meanings of spiritual teachings.

In Hinduism, to reach the goal of at-one-ment with the Godhead, one must learn how to move the ego aside. Spiritual exercises, such as analyzing spiritual literature and reflecting on its intentions, as well as meditation, are suggested to help us achieve detachment from ourselves and become one with what is eternal.

The Bible contains many warnings against pride. Pride goes before destruction is one of its famous maxims. (DT 9:4-6; Proverbs 16:18; Isaiah 2:17, 13:11; Jeremiah 50:31-32; Ezekiel 16:49-51; Obadiah 1:3-4)

The Bible's authors remind us that God is drawn to the humble. Those who are humble bare all their soul to God, seek His saving guidance and absorb His ready love. (2 Chronicles 7:14; Psalm 51:16-17; Isaiah 57:15, 66:2; Micah 6:8) Biblical law requires that even kings be humble and not expand their power or wealth excessively. (DT 17:14-20; Psalm 2:10-11) Moses was called the humblest man on Earth. (NU 12:3) He told us to circumcise our hearts – in other words, to be humble and self-limit our desires.

The soul communicates with the subconscious. The soul knows it needs humility in order to prepare for life in the spiritual realm. So, if we are being too pride-filled, our soul, in self-defense, may lead us to make decisions that will bring us to a humbling experience. One reason a sickness or injury may develop in us or a loved one is as a response to our subconscious spiritual goal to develop humility and empathy. Spiritually, we know that we cannot fully perceive God's guidance until we reduce our ego and seek God. Being humbled by poor health or circumstances can help us achieve that essential goal. As it is said in Ecclesiasticus (2:5, in the Apocrypha) as gold is tested in the fire, the God seeking are tested in the fire of humiliation.

Jesus called this pruning. (JN 15:1-2; and see Proverbs 3:11-12, 12:1, 5:23) We should be thankful when we are pruned, since it is ultimately more desirable to achieve the condition of humility while we are here than to be missing that spiritual advantage when we go to the other side of life.

It may be that the only thing keeping someone who has lived an exemplary life from returning to God's place is that they must be humble. Perhaps they are proud of their good deeds. So their spirit leads them to a humbling event or illness, a tragedy in the eyes of others. But if they can weather that humbling experience with love and praise for God – like the victim in Psalm 22, like Job, who lost all, and like Jesus, humiliated and tortured on the cross – it may be that they will fulfill all that is necessary to return to the place beyond time and substance and live eternally with God.

Look up at the night sky – and really look at it, long and deep. Think about stars, galaxies, planets – everything in motion and yet perfectly choreographed. Think about the genome, how it defines every element, and how perfectly it works. Do you feel humble in the presence of the One Who designed and created all that? Now meditate on what is beyond the universe of time and substance – God's kingdom – and you'll get a glimpse of how far we have come in separating ourselves from God by choosing our will over God's will. Humility opens us up to communication from the Great Spirit Who is waiting for our wall of pride to fall so It can lead us to submission and love -- life for our souls.

HUMILITY EXPERIMENT

Abraham, a "prince," left the comforts and conveniences of city life to seek God. He became a wanderer and tent dweller. Humbling himself by living in a tent and setting himself apart from the distractions of city life, Abraham meditated on and experimented with spirituality, sensitizing himself to perceive and interpret God's guidance. While

151

enduring the disadvantages of tent life, he steadied his resolve through the years and, step by step, turned his mind and spirit toward the One Almighty God, Creator of Heaven and Earth. He learned how to receive God's communications to him and trained himself to choose God's will over his own. Then, as God guided him, he adjusted the code of behavior for interpersonal and religious practices he had learned while growing up.

When his descendants, the Hebrews, left Egypt, they all took their tents with them. (LV 23:42-43; EX 16:16; DT 1:27, 5:30) They lived in their tents for 40 years. In the Bible we are told that for at least one week every year we are to live in a "moveable shelter," or tent. This is a humbling experience, because when we are in a fragile tent we are more dependent on God than ever for our safety and basic needs. It has the potential to be a strengthening and sharpening experience as well, because from it we can gain mental agility through innovation, and confidence through meeting the many small and large challenges of camping out. Through it we can develop self-confidence, self-sufficiency and adaptability. We also can learn to respect and live in harmony with nature instead of treating it carelessly and forcing our will against it.

Succoth is a harvest festival for seven days every autumn. This festival, sometimes called the Feast of Booths or Feast of Tabernacles, comes in the middle of the seventh lunar month of the year.

This experiment is to stay in a moveable shelter for the seven days of Succoth. (EX 23:16; LV 23:42-43) It is a humbling experience to live in a tent and be dependent on God for safety, sustenance and comfort. Even if it is a small tent set up in your living room or in your backyard, keeping this festival will help you collect camping gear and skills over the years and develop a closer relationship to the order God created in nature. Living simply in a tent for a week once every year gives us a humble perspective we carry with us for the rest of the year.

The Feast of Shelters is the inspiration for week long county and state fairs with their produce prizes, animal contests, games, crafts, shows, special foods and congregation of neighbors and relatives. It is a week-long festival of praising and thanking God, trading information and goods, learning ever more survival skills and sealing preparations for the long winter. It's a time to put aside your diet, relax, have fun and share your bounty with your religion's teachers and with those in need. The first and seventh days of this festival should be days of rest. Religious services on these days should be dedicated to thanksgiving and praise for God.

Decorations suggested in the Bible for the Feast of Shelters include, "the fruit of goodly trees" (usually interpreted as a citrus fruit) and "branches of palm trees and boughs of leafy trees, and willows of the brook." (LV 23:39-40) Unleavened bread or crackers, or a cup of flour with salt and olive oil, and a container with juice of the grape might be included, as in the Sabbath. A LED safety light or flashlight could be used instead of a candle.

If you have never camped out before, you might start off by pitching a small tent in your living room. Collect all the items you would need for a week of camping. Plan to use only your bathroom for convenience. (Commercial campgrounds have showers and bathrooms, as do many state and national parks that offer camping facilities.) During the week, keep two lists – one of items you forgot, and one of items you might eliminate. Add or scale down in the future. Eat outdoors, and sleep in your tent for the whole week.

After you are comfortable with living room tenting, in another year you might try a week in your fenced backyard. (Even in a suburban area an unfenced yard may sometimes host raccoons, coyotes or wild dogs.) If you have children, and they are old enough to follow your instructions, you might later try a camping experience in a commercial campground -- that is not in an area that has bears, wolves, coyotes or poisonous snakes. A young child is a tempting target for a quick, hungry bear, wolf or coyote. Older children, who understand safety skills and the importance of *not* feeding wild animals, can accompany you to state or national parks and, eventually, even to primitive camping.

Wherever you camp out, always think of safety first and exercise an abundance of caution. Learn about wild animals that live in and near where you will camp. Even if camping in your yard, if you have a baby, you might put up a tall fence to keep out neighborhood dogs and the wild animals that inhabit cities and suburbs. If a small animal such as a rodent scratches your tent in the middle of the night, shine a flashlight at that spot and it will probably leave.

Don't forget the basic do's and don'ts of camping out. Do wear long sleeves and slacks to minimize contact with stinging bugs and poisonous plants, and head gear to protect from ticks, spiders, etc. that fall from trees. Learn to identify poison ivy, oak and sumac. If you do get a skin rash or blisters, add a few drops of water to salt and rub the salt paste into the rash or blisters to clean out the oil that causes the rash. (Except, of course, don't use salt too close to your eyes.) Rub the salt in two or three times a day and let it dry before you brush it off. Not only will the rash not itch, it will dry up in a couple of days.

The symptoms of Lyme Disease, which is caused by tiny deer ticks, includes a bite that looks like a bull's eye target, a rash on the back of your neck, flu like fever and sniffles and perhaps headaches and pain in your joints. Consult a doctor if you have any of these symptoms and counteract them with antibiotics to avoid the severe arthritis that develops from the tick bite.

Be careful to keep a constant check on the weather while you are camping. Sudden intense rain in an area close to

154

your camping place – or in an area where rain drains close to your camping place -- could result in dangerous flash flooding that could carry away your tent and vehicle – and yourself. Don't set up your tent in a dry creek or river bed. It could flood suddenly. Do dig a small trench around the tent, so that in light rain the water will drain away from you. Put a rain fly and tarp over the tent and a tarp on the floor inside, in case rain leaks in. You should inform someone with whom you are in regular contact where you will be camping and for how long. If you are gone too long, they should alert rescuers.

Do pack a flashlight and batteries, first aid kit, radio with batteries, whistle, plenty of drinking water, an emergency signaling device and a map of the area where you will be camping. (Two long, two short, two long from your flashlight or whistle is a distress signal.) You might also need extra heavy blankets, warm clothes, rain gear, games or reading material.

If using a sleeping bag, you should turn it over each morning to dry condensation on its underside. Don't cover young children with a space blanket, or any plastic and aluminum blanket; they could slip under it and suffocate.

Don't drink water directly from creeks, streams, rivers or rain water catches. No matter how clear the water looks, it is not clean enough to drink without being filtered and boiled for five to ten minutes. If you are out of water and close to a stream or creek, dig a hole a few feet away from it and let water filter into the hole. Filter that again through a cotton cloth or by letting it settle overnight and pouring off the top one fourth to use. Boil this for five to ten minutes before drinking. If you are doing primitive camping, you should have a trowel with your gear to dig a latrine and fill it in with dirt after use. Don't put the latrine closer than 200 feet from a creek or river.

Handy food items include powdered drinks, dried fruits and nuts, crackers, peanut butter, hard candy and meat jerky. Dehydrated meals are efficient but require clean water and cooking utensils. All food should be in jars with screw tops. It's important to take everything away from your campsite that you take to it, so you may not want to take too many canned goods or disposable containers.

Don't keep any food in or near your tent. That could attract dangerous large and small animals. If your car is not close by, you could use a rope and hang food in a bag from a tree limb. Likewise, don't have the smell of food on yourself or your clothes when you go to bed. Wash your hands and brush your teeth so you don't smell like food and attract animals.

Don't leave food unattended on a table or picnic blanket. Small animals that carry rabies could handle the items and pass along the germs if their saliva gets into your mouth, an open sore or wound, or your eyes or nose. Because an animal may be infected without showing symptoms, this is also a reason to never feed wild animals.

When cooking food, go slow and be cautious. Read all instructions and warnings on fire starter packaging. If you are making a fireplace, don't use river rocks – they might explode. Fire starter squares are easy to carry and safe to use. **Never** squirt or douse a live fire with lighter fluid or kerosene, because the flame could spread instantly back up the stream and explode the container in your hand. Use water and dirt to completely extinguish the fire before you leave or retire for the night.

It's a good idea to learn about wild plants. Some berries taste good but are deadly poisonous. Don't ever eat a wild plant, even if it looks like a safe commercial variety, without positively identifying all its parts – its roots, stem, leaves, flowers, fruit and seeds. Everything must match the description of a safe plant. There are some deadly look-alikes.

Even though you build skills and confidence over the years, camping will always be a humbling experience. You are at the mercy of the weather, animals, insects, unexpected events and your own ignorance. Seek God's close guidance before, during and after this experiment and keep a journal of useful lessons learned.

SELF-DEFENSE

Every soul comes into the material realm for a purpose. Our instinct for survival comes from our soul's awareness that we have a purpose to fulfill and spiritual tests to meet here in order to develop skills and strengths to take back to the spiritual realm.

Though some would say that humans are at the top of the food chain and without predators, that isn't entirely true. War, disease, bad products, and false or missing information can kill us before we have completed our purpose for coming. Humans are sometimes predators to one another. A law of our spiritual nature is to protect the opportunities we have for life here and attempt to survive until we have completed the spiritual learning and balancing that we came here to do.

Confucius taught that a noble person, being virtuous, has no anxiety, being wise, is not perplexed and being courageous, has no fear. (A. 14.30) A noble person may indeed find himself in dire straits, but only a crude man becomes emotionally disturbed by it, he said. (A. 13.26-27)

The Buddha maintained that to be safe we should avoid disputes. Don't desire anything. Don't promote any doctrine. Don't engage in gossip. Don't argue or fight, if you would be safe, he said. Any action that disturbs another person's peace or harmony is sinful.

The book of Proverbs in the Bible is full of diplomatic advice. A mild answer turns away wrath. Sharp words stir up anger. (15:1) Watch kept over mouth and tongue keeps the watcher safe from harm. (21:23) The way of uprightness leads to life. The ways of the vengeful lead to death. (12:28) Mastery of temper is high proof of intelligence; a quick temper makes folly worse than ever. (14:29) Turn your back on the mouth that misleads; keep your distance from lips that deceive. (4:24)

Paul said, don't let the sun go down on your anger. (Ephesians 4:26, 31-32) For our own physical and spiritual self-defense, we must put away bitterness and malice, resolve disputes with diplomacy whenever possible, and create ways to live so as to not victimize others or be victimized by them.

Muhammad said, you may kill me, but I will not kill you, because I fear Allah, Who cherishes all people. But if you kill me, you will draw my sins on yourself and add them to your own, and when you die you will be tormented in the fire. (S. 4:92, 5:28-29)

About war Muhammad said, defend yourself only if you are attacked unjustly. (S. 26:227) If you die defending your religious beliefs, God forgives many of your sins. (S. 3:157) Similarly, Jesus said that those who lose their life in his service, save it. (MT 10:39)

Nevertheless, martyrdom is not a free pass to heaven. According to the Bible, our return to God's place hinges on living by the laws that govern spiritual nature until they are written on our hearts, and on submitting daily to God's guidance. (Jeremiah 32:37-40; MT 7:21-22) Only the Living Designer and Creator of the spiritual and material realms can lead each soul to opportunities to correct past errors and develop the spiritual strengths and skills it needs to succeed in the spiritual realm. So, it is crucial that we develop the spiritual sensitivity to perceive and choose God's will over our own willfulness. This takes time and effort and may require more than one life cycle. Someone who has been a martyr may be rewarded by reincarnating into comfort and ease in a future life, and yet be born with a very bitter attitude – because he or she wanted to go to heaven, not return to Earth.

People who live in a civilized environment have an aversion to murdering other people. In order to override that aversion in its most responsible citizens, a government and its media -- to suit a private agenda -- may systematically create a narrative that encourages citizens to disrespect and hate people in a nation that hasn't attacked them. By constantly repeating the narrative they build up their soldiers' desires to be protective, strong and courageous, as well as support for a war among their citizens. The clergy may support the effort by referring to where scriptures say that God directed people to go to war against nations whose citizens broke Fundamental Laws. This is a misuse of the Biblical accounts.

About four thousand years ago the Hebrews believed that God wanted them to wage war against idol worshippers because, besides breaking that law, they were breaking other important laws of spiritual nature. Some Bible interpreters point out that the Hebrews also needed a base from which to teach about the One Invisible God and God's Laws. A single base is no longer necessary because well over half of the people on Earth now worship in one of the three Abrahamic religions. What is needed now is for people everywhere to examine and live by the tenets of their faith and to engage in dialogue with those who seek to learn more about it. There is no holy or moral reason for war other than self-defense when being attacked. There is no reason to kill people who merely hold a different point of view about religion. We are each responsible before God for our own choices. Our responsibility is to seek out spiritual guidance for ourselves and to be good witnesses of our beliefs to others. In order to avoid wars for economic reasons, we must develop sustainable economic practices.

Jesus told us to not resist evil. Turn the other cheek, go the extra mile, give, rather than fight a thief. (MT 5:39-42) Revenge should be limited to using the legal system. Law enforcement services and courts exist to help us respond to personal threats and attacks. When they are inadequate, the person in error will still lead himself or herself to correction as their own spirit seeks to balance according to the laws of spiritual nature. Two wrongs won't make a right. To overreact to a perceived threat, or to respond with violence to verbal abuse or a physical attack that does not result in serious injury, will bind us to our attacker. Counseling, appeasement and moving away from a dangerous situation are all ways we could respond to direct threats to our emotional or physical safety.

The Bible tells several stories that relate to self-defense. Jacob appeased Esau – his brother, who had vowed to kill him – by sending him gifts and bowing humbly before him. (GN 32:7-22, 33:8-11)

Abigail sent an expensive gift of food to discourage David from attacking her husband. (1 Samuel 25:2-19)

Laban and Jacob made a treaty, after Jacob left Laban's service without notice. (GN 31:43-54) Abraham and Abimilech made a treaty about the well that Abraham's servants dug in Beersheba. (GN 21:22-32)

Traveling from Egypt, the Hebrews promised to stay on the King's Highway. They were still denied passage through Edom. Though able to fight, they didn't insist on their own way. Rather than provoke conflict, they turned aside. (NU 20:14-21)

Peter was rebuked by Jesus when he tried to defend him in the Garden of Gethsemane. (JN 18:10-11) Though confused, he did as he was told.

On the other hand, Abraham fought and rescued his nephew Lot and his family when they were taken from Sodom by raiders. (GN 14:11-16) Not all challenges can be resolved without force.

Some practices that help keep the peace include: to make a treaty, give gifts of appeasement, move to avoid conflict and don't provoke conflict.

Jesus said to shun the unrepentant, and to let the blind lead the blind. Though we should love our neighbors, it does their souls no good if we honor them while they victimize ourselves and others. They put their own future in danger by breaking the laws of spiritual nature. Shunning, instead of stoning, is a gentle reproof that may yet yield a change in their behavior.

Muhammad said, don't support in any way those who reject God's message. (S. 28:86, 4:140) Muhammad taught that goodness and evil cannot be equal. Repel evil with what is better, he said. Then your enemies might be changed into friends. (S. 41:34, 23:96)

Similarly, because the Moabites and Ammonites caused the Hebrews to sin, and also because they refused to sell them food and water, God told the Hebrews to not seek their peace or prosperity. (DT 23:3-6) Then, many generations later, the Moabitess Ruth, who kept the Law of Moses, married a Hebrew and became an ancestor of Israel's second king, David. By living by the rules of the One God, an enemy became a friend.

Through the Bible's writers, God bids us to help all those who have emergency needs. If you see that a neighbor needs emergency help, you should help him. (DT 22:4) If you see that someone who hates you needs emergency help, you should help him. (EX 23:5) We also should protect the opportunities for others to pursue their positive spiritual missions whether they are friends or enemies.

We are responsible for our own lives, as well as the lives of others. (GN 9:5) We are charged to protect not just our own opportunities to fulfill our spiritual purpose here, but also to respect the opportunities of others by making the world a safer place for us all. We show respect for others by not intruding unnecessarily in another's spiritual journey, and by exercising restraint and not creating destructive products or systems.

Confucius said that a noble person doesn't forget what is fair when he has an opportunity to make a profit. (A. 16.10) He also helps those who are destitute, and doesn't add to the wealth of those who are already rich. (A. 6.3) Following Confucius' advice one would not choose making a profit over providing a safe product for consumption, a fair economic system, or environmentally sustainable practices.

If you owned an island and built on it a fort stocked with food and weapons, you would still be vulnerable to a hungry mob, as well as a toxic germ. To be secure in the material realm, we must work toward spiritual security and work to help our neighbors with their security needs.

The antidote for fear is to be spiritually secure. If you are living every day preparing yourself for when you transition to the spiritual realm, your fears shouldn't be so great that you override another person's rights.

Part of becoming spiritually mature is wrestling with the tough decisions of how to make the larger social systems secure without crushing the micro systems of personal relationships. Engaging with the tensions of this challenge help us meet goals for spiritual life as well as material life.

162

SELF-DEFENSE EXPERIMENT

Look for ways you can contribute to helping everyone have their basic needs met. Some of these ways are mentoring children after school, mentoring new small business owners and being politically involved to bring about a more just economic system and an end to racial discrimination. Research the many public service organizations already available, then pick a project or create your own. Whatever helps build your community will help you feel safer.

WORK

In Hinduism karma is considered spiritual work. It is the law of cause and effect that is at work in every person's life. Our spirits are constantly at work trying to balance our thoughts, words and actions against the fixed laws of the spiritual realm. Everyone's ultimate goal is to learn spiritual lessons and escape the limitations of the material realm. Hindus teach that service to God – seeking to be an instrument of God – is one of the Four Paths one may take to achieve liberation. It is not work for money or honors. It is service as an instrument of God.

In Revelation 3:14-19 in the Bible, we are told that an angel visited a church in Laodicea. The Christians there were comfortably well off and self-satisfied. They weren't committing any sins. However, by not working to make a positive contribution to their community, they were by default letting destructive momentum become stronger. So, the angel said, it would spew them out. Work isn't just something we do to survive. It is also something we do, after seeking God's advice, to contribute to the spiritual well-being of our community and to develop ourselves mentally, emotionally and spiritually.

In the Ten Commandments we are told to work for six days, and rest on the seventh. We were not created for perpetual, selfish time wasting. We are responsible for making a contribution to our family and community by taking a job, creating a job or volunteering for a job. (DT 5:12-14; EX 23:12; LV 23:3)

A healthy body, mind and spirit naturally desires to make things better for their family and society, and there is always much that needs to be done. Something in us constantly seeks to build safer, more comfortable housing, provide food more efficiently and securely, stay or become healthy, and improve services and products for the needy and for the next generation. Even those who are wealthy find life more fulfilling if they are engaged in some type of work for the community. To not be making some sort of contribution is boring and depressing.

A saying attributed to Confucius is to choose a job you love, and you'll never have to work a day in your life. Working at a job you enjoy is a blessing.

If you seek a paying job, searching for the perfect, or even a comfortable, job can be frustrating. Nevertheless, there are actions even disappointed job seekers can take. First, by volunteering you can show that you are dependable and want to support the community. This will give you good references. It also will help you expand your network of acquaintances, who can tell you if they hear about a job or education program that can help you.

There are many ways to get training that will help you move from one vocation to another. Ask at an unemployment office or your library. Check the Internet, where scholarships for a variety of training programs are listed.

If you want to start a small business, your city may have a mentor program that can match you with a business man or woman who can counsel you for free. There also are programs that help small businesses get start-up funding. Crowd funding (on the Internet) is a way that some small businesses have gotten money to start producing a product or providing a service.

To begin a business, whether for profit or not for profit, you will need to register it with your state's Secretary of State office. There may be a registration form at your state government's website. A legal aid office, a mentor and just searching the Internet can help you find the information you need to fill out the application. Your library is also an excellent source of information, as there are many books that explain how to start and manage a business. One of these, *Give and Take, a Revolutionary Approach to Success,* by Adam Grant, explains the great importance of networking to business success.

It's very important to keep a positive attitude about job seeking and employment – even if it is a stepping stone job. If several people of equal experience have applied for the same job, the one with the best attitude has the best chance of getting hired and keeping the job. Exercise, social involvement, getting counseling from your religious teachers, prayer, singing, reading inspirational literature and avoiding artificial flavors (depressants) in what you eat can help you develop a positive attitude and weather the stress of working at finding or creating the job you want.

Through the process of job seeking or creation you will gain empathy for others you meet who also are seeking employment. This tender perspective should stay with you for many years and flavor your attitude when you become an employer or a mentor yourself.

In the Bible it is said that God's power is shown through our weakness. When we are comfortable and self-satisfied we aren't weak enough to dig deep for spiritual guidance. If we dare to ask God, during listening prayer, to guide us we may be challenged out of our comfort zone – but we may also come closer to trusting the power in the spiritual realm and learning how to submit to God. In order to fulfill our mission of learning spiritual skills and strengths while we are here, we should dare to be less comfortable and more zealous in seeking and doing. When we intently seek spiritual guidance, we make ourselves vulnerable and may be pushed out of our comfort zone to meet the challenges to which we are led.

Muhammad said, if you are doing work God guides you to do, don't worry about anyone who mocks you. God doesn't give any soul a burden it can't carry. (S. 7:42) Jesus was not accepted in his home city of Nazareth, and many of the respected Pharisees of his day rejected his interpretation of the scriptures. (LK 4:16-30; MT 13:54-58) Nevertheless, he continued to teach all who would listen, because God told him to. Moses didn't have a comfortable reign either. Though God had worked many miracles through him, he still faced rebellion within his camp, and even within his family. So, don't worry about criticism you may receive for a job you want to do or need to do. If it is legal and moral, and you believe God led you to it, seek what you can learn from it.

The political atmosphere of today is such that it is often dangerous to be openly God-centered. Conservatives get heckled at restaurants, are victims of rocks and insults when they hold public meetings, are treated unfairly by social media and the press and are passed over for jobs and advancements in some offices. In some countries they are brutally attacked, killed, or arrested on spurious charges and imprisoned. Nevertheless, part of the work of every religious person is to keep God in the conversation as we go about our daily tasks -- to acknowledge God and talk about God with others. This may create conflict for us, but it is our job to conform the world to the laws of the spiritual realm, not conform ourselves to the rebellious world. If we do not keep God in the conversation, then by default we let the world devolve into selfishness and iniquity.

WORK EXPERIMENT

Always use listening prayer to determine where and how God wants you to invest your time, talents and resources. Then work at something that makes a contribution to your community. Have a goal. Help a neighbor. If you can't find an organization whose mission you agree with, create one yourself.

If you do volunteer work, investigate non-profits before you pick one to support. Some non-profits write a compelling mission statement, but they exist to make money and not to fulfill their mission.

Also, it is a waste of money to donate to a third party instead of directly to the organization you wish to support. Even if you designate who you wish the money to go to, there is no guarantee your money will go there and the third party also has to cover office expenses, which can be significant. Often organizations whose values are not your own get funded this way.

Those charities that raise money by telephoning potential donors typically use 85% of the money they collect for themselves. Only 15% goes to the cause for which they are soliciting. You can verify with your Secretary of State the percent of money the charity gives to their stated mission. Also, ask the recipients for whom they are collecting money how much aid they have received from the collection organization. If possible, visit their offices and learn first-hand if the collection organization dispenses donations responsibly, and if they are dedicated to their stated mission.

Reaching out to help others is an important teaching in the Christian religion. If you are a Christian, there are many wonderful opportunities to be involved with volunteer work through your church. Walk into almost any Christian congregation on their Sabbath day and at the time of announcements they will probably offer ongoing, organized community service opportunities. These projects stretch out into the community and include Christians and non-Christians alike. Many churches have programs that feed the hungry, support shelters for the homeless, help build Habitat for Humanity houses, staff thrift stores, and more. A church may also adopt a church in another country and send it supplies, money and literature. Through the church you may become politically involved to promote Christian values in society, learn counseling skills, help with the church's children's programs, help with church maintenance, visit the sick or work in other ways.

CHAPTER SIX

PREPARING FOR WHAT COMES NEXT

In order for a functioning, interdependent, and ultimately life protecting, universe to evolve randomly – even if it could, which is disputed – it would take an infinite amount of time. In 1927 Monseigneur George Lemaitre proposed the theory that the universe was created with a big bang, and not by infinite random evolution. In 2016 the Big Bang Theory was given significant support from results of tests at CERN's Large Hadron Collider. Scientists now date the universe as being about 13.7 billion years old – much too short a time for it to have been created by random evolution. Over the years, a huge quantity of supporting data for the Big Bang Theory has come from widely different scientific sources. Today, the overwhelming majority of astrophysicists accept the soundness of the Big Bang model of the universe.

Astrophysicist Hugh Ross said (concerning the creation of functioning human biology) "Statistical mechanics tells us…the greater the complexity and functionality of a system, the less advantageous additional time becomes for assembly by random processes (the parts wear out too soon)." In his book, *The Creator and the Cosmos: How the Latest Scientific Discoveries of the Century Reveal God*, he explains in detail how much more true this is of the exquisitely balanced, functional universe, for which laws applied to materials have brought about a specific, organically developed design.

Even if there is a field that is neither matter nor energy and that both carries within it all the laws of our universe and compels how those laws are applied to materials, as some suggest, this would still be according to a specific design. If such a field could cause the systems and objects that come into being in the universe, in the end it would still leave us with the questions: Who designed and created that field, all the laws and materials within it, compelled them into motion in the Big Bang and continues to sustain that motion?

The obvious answer is that there must be a Living, Intelligent Designer. *Something* created laws and applied them – or designed and created a field that applies them – according to a specific order, unfolding according to a specific, organic design. Because laws imposed on materials according to a design exist, there must be something that caused that. This something is Omniscient, Omnipotent and Alive. Expand your mind and try to take in the magnitude of God's power, presence – and purpose. What could be so powerful and all-knowing that It could instantly create the single design, multitude of laws and materials and nests of organically adjusting systems found in this universe?

We call the Great Designer and Creator "God" and traditionally refer to God using the masculine pronoun, though in religious literature around the world God is described as having both masculine and feminine attributes. We know God exists because we can see the multidimensional order, precise balance and functionality of the ultimately life protecting world that God has designed and brought about.

For centuries, philosophers have tried to prove God's existence with logical arguments. But the way many people become convinced that God exists is by personally experiencing God's presence in their lives. When this happens, faith/trust becomes like a rock, something we can hold on to no matter what else happens in life. It's this personal experience that drives the religious.

While for some belief in God is grounded in experience, others close themselves off from recognizing the experiences of God's presence in their lives. Jesus could not perform many miracles in his home town of Nazareth, for example, because of their unbelief. (MT 13:58) It is necessary to have awakened one's spiritual sensitivity and then to have the courage to open up to spiritual communication in order to recognize God's presence. Once we have experienced God's presence, where God came from is not relevant. We are bound to respond to the reality of our experience.

After we acknowledge that a Living, Conscious, Creative Power has designed and brought into being the entire universe and everything in it, the obvious next question is: Why? What is the purpose of God's vast show of power and brilliance?

Hindus teach that God-seeking is our spirit's desire to return to a place in the spiritual realm where there is unending joy. Spiritually we are aware that it is possible to attain liberation from the sorrow, desperation, pains and boredom of material life. They say a way to achieve liberation comes after cleansing ourselves spiritually by living by Five Moral Principles, and by connecting with Brahma (the Godhead) through meditation. This is a form of repentance. We acknowledge that we are separate from God because of our errors -- and change, with the intent to live without error.

The emphasis on **repentance** and spiritual cleansing found in all of the civilization supporting religions of today is a clue that deep in our souls we are aware that we have erred and separated ourselves from the Creator of our souls. The universe, in all its great array and minute precision, is a testament to God's abiding love for us. Rather than extinguishing the rebels, God has created a place where we can recognize our mistakes and act to correct them.

The Bible's prophets of old were like the prophets of the polytheistic ancients in that they sought communication from the spiritual realm. The difference was that the Hebrew prophets showed respect for the Great Designer and Creator by seeking God's will over their own rather than by trying to force their will over God's.

Noah listened to God, and then built an ark, stocked it with food and locked the animals and his family inside for seven days before the rain began. (GN 6:8, 13-22) Abraham sought communication with God through the oracle at the Oak of Mamre in Shechem. (GN 12:6 TNJB, IB) There he learned how to perceive God's guidance, and chose it again and again. Moses found an oracle in a burning bush and learned how to receive God's guidance regularly. (EX chapter 3) God spoke "face to face" with Moses, guided him in delivering the Hebrews from Egypt and told him to write the Law He wanted those who worship the One Almighty God to live by. Jesus said that he said and did only what God told him to say and do. (JN 12:49) Muhammad went to a secluded place and fasted to receive inspiration and guidance from God and to create *The Holy Qur'an*.

What these sensitive leaders perceived is that our Creator has an agenda, a reason behind the vast show of power and brilliance that is the cosmos in all its functioning detail. God's Master Plan is that all who are separated from God learn love for and submission to our Designer and Creator so we may return to a place beyond time and substance where we will live eternally with God. That Abraham sought and followed the guidance of the Living Designer, Creator Spirit, and taught others all he learned about the One God of Heaven and Earth, has furthered that Plan. The Bible tells us that all the nations on Earth will be blessed as a result of Abraham's teachings, which have spread all over the world and impacted religions other than the three Abrahamic religions. (GN 18:17-19)

Moses furthered that Plan by writing down rules of behavior he discerned through communication with the Holy Spirit. Part of that is what is called the Ten Commandments. Many of the rules in the Ten Commandments had already been practiced for centuries by all of the largest societies in the ancient world. But two of its rules are unique: the Seventh Day Sabbath of complete rest and the law to not bow to an idol.

The law against idol worship was a major break with the religions of the ancient Middle East. It was simply social protocol to pay one's respects to the local deity of whatever city or state one visited by offering a sacrifice and bowing to the deity. Everyone did it. It was a social nicety that said, basically, that you came in peace. When God forbade the Hebrews from this practice it was a social slap in the face to all the other nations in the region.

The nations of the Middle East were in awe of the Hebrews because they had heard of the Hebrews' miraculous release from slavery in Egypt. They wondered, who were these people who thought their God was the only True God, and an invisible God at that?

God was setting the Hebrews up to be a nation with the mission to lead the world back to acknowledgement and **submission to the Designer and Creator of the spiritual and material realms**. So, they were told to burn to destruction all the statues in the country God had designated for them. They were being given a base of operations from which to lead the world.

Nevertheless, several hundred years after the Hebrews settled in Canaan, and because of social pressure from the people who survived their takeover of the land, some Hebrews struggled with staying true to the law against idol worship. Some intermarried with polytheists and allowed idols in their homes.

The human propensity to worship what we can see, and to follow peer pressure without question, bedevils every generation. Today the pressures of social nicety try to get us to prefer sexual deviancy, greed and power over the laws for self-discipline, honesty and loyalty. It is always a challenge to choose guidance from the Invisible Designer and Creator of the universe – Who we have to learn to communicate with by exercising our invisible spirit -- over lures and threats we can see and feel, as well as the social pressures created by those who are still in ignorance of, or in open rebellion against, the laws of spiritual nature.

There is a difference between believing in the spiritual realm and believing in the One, Invisible, All-Powerful, Ever-Living God. Primitive people who had experienced spiritual communication – sometimes with departed loved ones – knew that spirits had the power to advise those who remained in the material realm. Throughout the ancient world, humans sought communication with spirits on the other side of life. Some used magic, incantations, self-flagellation, candles, chants, music and sacrifices to drive themselves into a state of sensitivity where they thought they had a spiritual experience with their gods and might be able to convince their gods to intercede for them and aid events in their lives. They made statues representing them, made sacrifices to them and asked for favors from them. The use of oracles, divination and astrology developed as aids to communicate with the "gods," but these methods were undependable. In addition, one drawback to designating spirits of the dead as gods was that they retained the very human deficiencies of selfishness and violence.

The gods they tried to bribe were sometimes deceased rulers whom they deified, as is recorded in the ancient Egyptian and Hittite civilizations and in polytheistic Rome. A form of this practice crept into the Roman Catholic Church, which confers sainthood on some of its deceased leaders. Some Catholics pray to a saint instead of to God.

God, however, forbids us to have recourse to the spirits of the dead. (LV 19:31) We could. Spirits are alive after their bodies die. But the Spirit of God seeks to guide us. For us to pray to a departed saint, leader or relative is insulting to God, Who has all knowledge of people and events and Who seeks to guide us to what is ultimately best for each person's soul. In addition, those who are deceased should not be held back from continuing on their spiritual journey by being evoked in prayers.

In order for God's will be to done on Earth, which was taught by Abraham, Moses, Jesus and Muhammad -- and that Jesus said we should pray for (in the Lord's Prayer) -- we have to seek and submit to God's will daily. In order to perceive and interpret God's communications to us, we must develop **spiritual sensitivity** and employ "listening prayer," where we take all our concerns to the Living Designer and Creator of the spiritual and material realms, set aside our ego and listen without fear, but with expectation and desire, to receive God's response. This takes a little practice. A diet free of additives and salicylates as well as a lifestyle that practices the laws of spiritual nature help prepare us to have the honesty and courage to perceive God's ready guidance.

Hindu and Buddhist meditation practices, though they weren't developed to receive messages from God, might be useful in helping us disengage from distractions and connect with our spirit's Creator. Both religions teach that we must keep the laws that cleanse and discipline us spiritually before we can experience the benefits of meditation.

Muhammad cautioned that we should not pray with a fogged mind (meaning either drunk or under the influence of drugs) or when we are impure. (S. 4:43, 5:6) He also said we should seek God by using His wonderful names, and avoid people who use God's names abusively. Fear God and listen, Muhammad said, for God doesn't guide rebels. (S. 5:108)

In the song of Moses, it is said that God turns His face away and waits to see what will become of those who are disloyal to Him. (DT 32:18-20) This could be psychological projection. When we are disloyal to our Creator it is because we have turned away and refused to seek communication from the Living Spirit that created us. Because humans have free will, we have the ability to deny God's existence and block our spiritual perception of God's presence and communication.

In the Bible, God said He would destroy all on Earth because they had turned their backs and did not seek or consult God. (Zephaniah 1:2-7) Isaiah warned that those who don't seek God or listen to God's advice would be sorry. (Isaiah 30:1, 65:12) Jeremiah reminded us that God gave no law regarding sacrifice. His one command was, "Listen to My voice." (Jeremiah 7:22-23) Daniel confessed that the Jews hadn't listened to God's voice or followed His Law. (Daniel 9:9-11)

We can communicate with our Creator about anything, but we should do it respectfully. After the Hebrews had been safely and miraculously rescued from slavery, they complained about the harsh conditions they encountered during their travel through the desert. This ungrateful attitude drew correction to them. (NU 11:1-20, 31-34, 21:4-9; Isaiah 45:9) We are forbidden to curse God. (LV 24:10-16) Jesus went through many painful tests, but he didn't complain or curse God. On the cross, where it is reported that he said, "My God, my God, why hast Thou forsaken me..." he was likely quoting the well-known Psalm 22, which begins with that phrase and describes the effects of crucifixion, but ends with praise for God.

Many people in the ancient Middle East were drawn to learn more about the Invisible, Almighty God perceived by Abraham because there is no selfishness in God. Unlike the ever changing laws of the idols, which were interpreted by kings and priests to protect the rich at the expense of everyone else, the laws God gave were fair for all people and made provision and protection for the poor and weak. Also, the various laws of the God of Abraham were set. They didn't change when rulers changed. Seeking to please just one God, instead of a pantheon of gods who had power over different areas of life, also was an attractive alternative.

Still, it was challenging for polytheists to change and commit to a single invisible God. Muhammad said that God is too great to see. God has power over all and is aware of all that transpires, he said. He also said that God is closer than your heartbeat. (S. 6:103, 50:16, 8:24) It was intriguing to some, and frightening to others, that God could see their thoughts and secret acts and might communicate with them anywhere.

Muhammad taught that Allah is One, Eternal and Absolute. He had no birth, and He didn't beget one like Him. There is no one like God. (S. 112:1-4) Don't make a person an object of worship with Allah; I am warning you, he said. (S. 51.51) Muhammad said that if someone expects to meet God, he should live a righteous life and not admit a partner when he worships God. (S. 18:110)

Jesus would agree. He said that blasphemy against the Holy Spirit (i.e., calling a human or an object by God's name, or ascribing God's power to a person or object) is an unforgivable sin. (MT 12:31) Jesus taught that God is Spirit, that God is One, and that we must love the One God completely. (JN 4:24; MK 12:28-32) He spoke of himself as separate from God dozens of times throughout the gospels. When he used the "I am" phrase he said, "ego emi," a natural way anyone would use to say "I am." He never referred to himself as YHWH, the ineffable name of God that Moses perceived, and that some interpreters think might mean, "I Am." (EX 3:14-15) Hebrew was originally written without vowels, so it is uncertain what word the four letters refer to – or whether, indeed, it is an acronym for four words. Some believe it is a third person form and could mean, "He causes to be." Others conjecture that it could mean "I am what I am," as a way of saying that God is too great for us to understand. It is also interpreted as "I create," "I am eternal" and "I am because I am." (T, OAB, IB, TNJB)

When a man called Jesus "good," he objected and said that only God is good. (LK 18:19) He said that only God knows

177

when tribulation will come (MT 24:36) that two witnesses are required, and that he is one and God is the other one (JN 8:17-18) that by himself he could do nothing (JN 5:19, 10:37-38, 12:49, 14:10) that he didn't come of his own accord (JN 7:28-29) that he was not alone but God was with him (JN 8:16, 16:32) and that the Father is greater than he. (JN 14:28) In the Garden of Gethsemane he said, "Thy will be done," though his will, initially, had been different. (MT 26:39, 42) The foundation of Islam is loyalty and submission to the One Great Spirit that creates the spiritual and material realms, and life itself. (S. 22:38, 4:125) Jesus would agree.

He said that his mother, brothers and sisters are those who hear the word of God and do it. (MT 12:50) By claiming that he is our brother he is accentuating that he is distinct from God and one with those whom God created. We have returned to the family of God when we learn to perceive and choose God's will over our own, the way that Jesus did.

Though Jesus is a *holy* son of God, he isn't the *only* son of God. We have only to look at the Lord's Prayer, where he told us to say, "**Our Father** which art in heaven..." to verify this. (MT 6:9; LK 11:2) God is the Father (and Mother) of us all. The Song of Moses says that God turned away because of the provocation of His sons and His daughters. (DT 32:19) Isaiah twice called God our Father. (Isaiah 63:16, 64:8) Jesus said that peace makers will be called sons of God. (MT 5:9) The apostle John said that to whoever received him, Jesus gave them the power to *become* the sons of God. (JN 1:12) After his resurrection Jesus said he was going to "my Father and your Father, and to my God and your God." (JN 20:17) Jesus desired that his disciples be one with him and God. He also said he desired that all on Earth become children of light. (JN 17:6-25, 12:36) Paul said that all who are led by the Spirit of God are the sons of God. (Romans 8:14) That we are all God's children is a recurring theme in the Bible. Our goal is to return to our Creator as submissive children. (LK 20:37-38) Jesus, who was like us, tells us and shows us the way.

God made us with free will, with the capacity to exercise choice, to communicate creatively, to express loyalty and forgiveness and to learn and apply invisible laws. We are designed to be able to perceive and respond to guidance from our invisible Creator, though we must of our own free will choose to do so. Where much has been given, much is expected. We are expected to choose to be led by the Spirit of God to do God's will. When we do this we are behaving as responsible children of God.

Jesus said that everyone who believes him -- that is, who commits to live by his teachings -- will have everlasting life. He also said that God's wrath stays on anyone who does not commit to (be obedient to) him. (JN 3:36) When we choose the lures and threats of the material realm over spiritual teachings, we close ourselves off from the mental and behavioral patterns that would lead us to develop spiritual sensitivity and prepare for what comes next. Spiritual teachings and examples show us how to prepare for our inevitable life in the spiritual realm – but it is we who decide when to take into ourselves the spiritual food and drink of those teachings and examples.

We should fill ourselves with spiritual food while we are here so we may live forever where we will never experience physical hunger or thirst again. Jesus said that his teachings are food for our spirit and his example is the living water, the life blood of social interactions. (JN 6:27-35, 40, 52-63) His uncomplaining submission to injustice and a gruesome death, followed by his glorious resurrection on the third day were examples of his love for humanity and his love and dedication to God that is meant to prove the reality of the spiritual realm and draw us to live by his teachings so we also experience God's presence and guidance in our own lives and succeed in being reborn into God's place beyond time and substance. (JN 12:32, 3:14-16)

We scarce can take it in, that a God of love and justice would allow one in whom He was "well pleased" to be humiliated, tortured and slowly murdered by crucifixion. But God loves every soul, and God's Master Plan is for every human soul to return to love and submission to its Designer and Creator. Jesus knew the Master Plan, and he agreed to fulfill the mission God had given him. He had tried to convince the religious leaders of his time to embrace their mission to teach about the love, laws and purpose of the All-Knowing, All-Powerful Spirit that creates Heaven and Earth to all people in all nations. God guides, but we have free will, and the leaders chose against their opportunity and mission. (LK 7:30)

Jesus knew what would happen next. He knew that, after his death, his resurrection would become a symbol that would prove to all on Earth that life continues in the spiritual realm, and that we can safely submit our lives to God when God guides us to face our fears and make choices for the good of all people, choices that further God's Plan to save every soul on Earth. The empty cross, a symbol of Jesus' resurrection, is a powerful symbol that the worst that can happen to us in the material realm is a passing thing. If we choose to develop spiritual sensitivity by employing the laws that govern spiritual nature, and respond to God's daily guidance with love and humility, then our life in the spiritual realm will be filled with love, peace, joy and satisfaction.

Jesus said that he and God make a home in those who live as Jesus taught. This is because when we become one in purpose with God by living the way Jesus taught and exampled, we absorb into ourselves that spiritual rhythm that is alive in the world. (JN 14:23-24)

It is hard for us to comprehend this Constant, Loving Presence amidst all the distractions, pressures, desires and fears of our everyday lives. We must conscientiously develop spiritual sensitivity so that, even at the pressure points of life, we can more easily discern God's presence and guidance and persevere in faith no matter what may befall us. Like Jesus – both in this realm and the spiritual realm -- we are safe in God's hands.

When people break the Fundamental Laws, it is because they don't understand that these are needed in order to enjoy the benefits of group living, and/or because they don't believe there is punishment currently or in a future life for law breaking. The way that Jesus' resurrection "took sin out of the world," was that it proved the existence of the spiritual realm and validated Jesus' teachings about how to prepare for it, clearing up misunderstandings about the importance of the need to live by the laws of spiritual nature.

When we live by Jesus' teachings to develop spiritual sensitivity and learn to perceive and submit to God's daily guidance, we experience the transformative power that comes from recognizing God's reality, presence and love. Then we learn how to correct the rebellion that separates us from our Creator and we become one will with and compatible with our Creator again. When we reverse our rebellion against our Creator and learn how to perceive and submit to God's daily guidance we don't sin, because all sin is choosing our will over God's will.

The reward – eternal life beyond time and substance with our Designer and Creator – does not come before obedience and submission to God, though it is eternally available to us. Salvation is for those who sensitize themselves to daily perceive and submit to God's will. This was the teaching of Abraham, Moses, Jesus and Muhammad.

God's promises are if/then. Like a contract, if one party does a promised thing, the other is bound to do their promised thing. God told the Hebrews that IF they lived by His laws AND submitted to His guidance (obeyed His "voice") THEN He would make them a nation of priests – a holy nation (on mission to the world). (EX 19:3-6; DT 26:16-19) The first level of demonstrated respect and love for God is obedience to the laws that govern spiritual nature. The fact that God included in His promises Abraham's slaves and, later, the Egyptians who left Egypt with the Hebrews, as well as all members of households where the male head of the household accepts circumcision, shows that everyone who chooses obedience is chosen by God.

How can we show complete love to the One God, the Great Designer and Creator Spirit Who has shown such steadfast and patient love for us? First, we can study and experiment with what those who were spiritually sensitive have revealed about the spiritual realm. If you want to learn about anything, you first study what others have already learned about it. Just as we don't have to create the whole field of mathematics for ourselves, we don't have to create the whole field of spirituality. It is written for us and we can validate it by applying its rules to our lives. After we have studied and experimented with the various laws of spiritual nature that God created, we show respect for God by continuing to be obedient to those laws.

If we apply the laws to be honest, humble and loyal in our relationships with one another we develop character qualities that carry over into our relationship with God. When we communicate honestly and with humility and loyalty with God, we can more easily perceive God's presence and guidance.

Praising our Creator and observing holy days weaves a rhythm of acknowledgement and respect for our Creator into our lives. This is also an expression of love for God.

The Bible tells us to not come before God without bringing an offering. (EX 23:15, 34:20; DT 16:16-17; 2 Samuel 24:24) One of the rules written in the Bible is to tithe. Tithing -- giving 10% of our before tax money to the religious institution from which we receive learning -- supports God's sanctuaries, priests and programs in society. This helps further God's soul-saving agenda. The tension of tithing draws us to take better care of our resources. In addition to the tithe, instead of the food sacrifices given by an agricultural people, when we want to celebrate a special occasion and thank God, we would give an additional gift to support God's soul-saving agenda.

It is interesting to note that Sikhism, a religion that blends aspects of Hinduism and Islam, teaches its adherents to tithe ten percent of their income to charities, a discipline that is taught in neither of the other two religions, though both teach the value of charitable giving.

Another way we show love to God and support God's Plan to save all souls on Earth is to talk about God wherever we are and push back with that light against the darkness of the self-first world. It is important to bring spiritual light into the lives of others and let them in on the joy they can experience even in the midst of injustice and hardship, and to explain how they can counteract temptations and dispel fear and sadness by employing the rules made by the One Who created the material and spiritual realms.

In these and other ways we show love to God -- and simultaneously develop spiritual sensitivity, so that when we employ listening prayer it is easier for us to perceive and interpret God's communications to us. Submitting to God's daily guidance is how we are drawn back into trusting God and becoming one in purpose with our Creator so we may prepare for what comes next after this life.

REPENTANCE

Gnosticism – which produced "gospels" created by inspiration rather than by witness or research -- taught that the material realm was created because some spirits rebelled against God. This inspired interpretation is also given in several places in the Bible. Adam and Eve's choice of their will over God's will is a symbol that our selfishness and willfulness separated our souls from Paradise, or

Heaven. (GN 3) In the Song of Moses, God complained that we turned from Him and chose our will over His, and that punishment followed. (DT 32) Psalm 82 relays that we were separated from Heaven because of our injustice and abuse of power.

Gnostics held that the material realm is a place from which souls have the opportunity to be saved by righteous living. This is an enduring belief from one religion to another. In Hinduism, for example, there are Four Paths to liberation from the cycle of reincarnation: knowledge (learning spiritual texts, and meditation) love and worship for God, working as God's instrument and exercises of self-discipline and meditation. So, for Hindus also the reason we are in this realm is to avail ourselves of opportunities to develop spiritual strengths and skills and to be liberated by righteous living.

In some sects of Hinduism it is said that souls with excessively bad karma go to one of seven layers of hell until they have repented and atoned for their sins. Nevertheless, Hindus say that atonement can be achieved in a person's current life by repenting and following actions prescribed by a priest. To live an ascetic life or to give charity, for instance, may be required.

When we acknowledge our Creator and learn the laws that govern the material and spiritual realms, it gives us joy and hope. We realize that both the material and spiritual realms are cause and effect and that it is possible to make better choices and cause better effects. We have the option to repent of having broken the laws of spiritual nature and change ourselves spiritually so that we may return to our Creator, Who forever loves each one of us. Jesus said that tax collectors and prostitutes were making their way into Heaven before the self-satisfied religious leaders -- because they repented but the others did not. (MT 21:28-32)

In the Bible it says that God forgives the humble repentant. In repentance we honestly confess that we have erred, and then we change our behavior. Since we have confessed and changed, we are no longer who we were before and we can accept God's guidance in meeting the tests and challenges we need to meet to rebalance spiritually. (DT 4:29-31; Isaiah 1:16-20; Jeremiah 18:1-12)

Muhammad agrees. If one repents, believes and does works of righteousness, God will turn the evil they did into good, he said. (S. 25:70, 6:54) Muhammad frequently said that Allah is most forgiving. He said that even those who have transgressed bounds, if they repent, establish regular prayers and practice regular charity, are to be accepted as brothers in the faith. (S. 9:11) If Allah punished everyone for their wrongdoing, no one would be left on Earth, he said. Allah gives respite until the time of punishment. (S. 16:61)

What may actually happen is that by changing – by making restitution where we can and by choosing to live according to the laws of spiritual nature -- we bring our spirit back into balance with what governs spiritual nature. (NU 5:5-8; LV 5:20-26) Then our negative experiences change and we experience "forgiveness." Because we have changed to live within the Law, our experiences change – sometimes abruptly, sometimes over a period of years as we continue to replace old habits and ways of thinking with better ones.

Though we may believe that we didn't do anything to incur a certain punishing experience that came to us, we have to allow for words and actions we could have taken in a previous life, as well as for the fact that new injustices occur in the social mix of life just because we are in materiality. We have all committed the initial error of choosing our will over God's that brought us into the material experience. While here we are vulnerable to the whole range of social and environmental experiences of material beings.

Jesus said that unless all repent, all will perish. (LK 13:1-5) We have all chosen our will over God's will, so we all need to repent and repair that broken trust. Everyone on Earth has chosen their will over God's will. We can see this attitude of selfishness and rebellion everywhere. All the injustice and evil in the world comes from humans choosing their will over God's will.

Nevertheless, God loves every soul faithfully. Whenever we choose to repent – to apologize for our errors, give up selfishness, forgive one another and live by the laws God created – we signal our own soul as well as God that we seek to return to obedience and submission to our Creator, and we begin the delicate process of re-learning how to become one in purpose with the Great Living Spirit that designed and created the universe and everything in it. When we change from being arrogant rebels to having the Law "written on our hearts" and to submitting to God, we experience reconciliation. Striving to be one in purpose with God, we become compatible with God and prepare to blend back into God's kingdom from which we came. Like the Prodigal Son, when we humbly repent God welcomes us back with great joy and celebration.

Thousands of years ago polytheists sacrificed things they loved – sometimes even a child – to show repentance. They used prayers, various kinds of fasts, sexual abstinence, wearing sackcloth, sleeping in ashes, martyrdom, blood sacrifices, scapegoats and other methods to apologize and seek forgiveness for their sins. They even re-wrote some of the scriptures they had received, as if that could change reality.

Some sought to be forgiven for breaking the rules of a deity by shedding the blood of an animal. The practice of pouring out an animal's blood as a symbol of one's life (blood) as a way to repent -- to rededicate one's life to follow the rules -- was widely practiced. The Hebrews also practiced this symbolism. (LV 17:10-11) However, it became lip service repentance. Many prophets, as well as Jesus, said that God wants justice and mercy, not sacrifice. (Proverbs 21:3; Hosea 6:6; Psalm 40:6-8; Jeremiah 7:22-23; Micah 6:6-8; Amos 5:21-24; Isaiah 1:10-17) Claiming that all sins – past, present and future (as some say) – are forgiven for those who acknowledge Jesus' death and resurrection, leads to the same lip service repentance. Many Christians wonder why they have to live a moral life if Jesus has already secured heaven for them by pouring out his blood.

We have always desired an easy way to get rid of guilt. One ancient practice was to place the sins of the community on the head of a live goat and send it away to a wild place – a scapegoat. This was so popular and widely practiced that it was picked up by the Hebrews and is still written in the Bible as part of the yearly Day of Atonement ritual. (Leviticus 16:21-22) On Easter Sunday, thousands of ministers and priests tell their congregants that Jesus' death on the cross takes away their sins. But look around. We can see that even Christians go right on sinning. Jesus is used like a scapegoat.

Just as people continued to sin even after they made all manner of sacrifices, they have continued to sin after participating in the yearly Day of Atonement -- and after acknowledging Jesus' death and resurrection. Jesus didn't intend for his sacrifice to wipe away our sins. Instead, it was his *example* of submitting to God's will, even to the point of death, followed by his resurrection that was intended to lead people to believe in the reality of the spiritual realm and prepare -- by following his instructions and example of complete submission to God -- to live in it. When we do that – when we recognize that we have someplace to prepare to go and change our lives so we may be ready for it after we die here – then sin is on its way out of our lives and the world.

Jesus told us to be branches from his vine, in other words to imitate him -- that is, to imitate his lifestyle of honesty, humility, obedience to the laws of spiritual nature, love for others and love and submission to God. (JN 15:1-6) We are charged to take up our cross daily and follow him. His message is that we must choose the laws of spiritual nature, as well as God's daily guidance, over material lures and threats.

The symbol created by Jesus' resurrection continues to reverberate down the centuries and around the Earth. Many are drawn to investigate Jesus' teachings and lifestyle because he resurrected after a brutal death and appeared to hundreds of his followers. (Acts 1:1-11, 1 Corinthians 15:3-8; LK 24:13-35; MK 16:9-11; JN 20:1-29)

After his resurrection, Jesus told his disciples to teach repentance for the remission of sins in his name to all nations. (LK 24:45-48) It is important that this was *after* he resurrected. Notice that he did not tell his disciples to preach that his death absolved anyone of their sins, or that because he had died and resurrected they could live however they pleased and still go to Heaven after their time on Earth. In order to have sins remitted we have to do something. We have to acknowledge our errors and change our lives. Forgiveness of sins is dependent on repentance – on confession and a changed life. Forgiveness doesn't come by paying lip service to a belief, by praising Jesus, or by being a member of the Christian religion.

Rather than expecting Jesus to magically wipe away our sins, living the way he taught us to live is the way to honor Jesus' life, because it furthers his mission to teach the world that God is Alive, loves us, and accepts us back when we repent and choose God's will over our own.

It starts with obedience. When a young man asked how to have eternal life, Jesus asked, "Do you keep the Law?" The first level of choosing God's will over our own is to be obedient to the rules God guided Moses to write that Jesus interpreted. There is no scapegoat, DNA marker or magic wand that takes away sin. We must humbly confess that we have erred, change our lifestyle and be obedient to the laws that govern spiritual nature. Forgiveness comes after we change from rebellion and selfishness back to obedience and choosing God's daily guidance. (LV 26:40-45; DT 30:1-10)

Paul sought to convert the polytheistic Greeks and Romans. He claimed that if they believed Jesus died on the cross and rose from the dead then their (past) sins would be atoned for because of Jesus' blood and because they believed. He then told them they would be held accountable for their future behavior. Paul's doctrine of easy atonement has been used to mislead many to believe that they can live however they want and still go to heaven if they acknowledge Jesus' death and resurrection. Many ministers choose to pacify their members with this doctrine and ignore Paul's many entreaties that Christians live a moral and self-disciplined life. (See 1 Corinthians 6:9-11, Galatians 5:16-26 and Ephesians 5:1-6)

John the Baptist and Jesus replaced the symbol of animal sacrifice for repentance with water baptism – total immersion in a running body of water -- as a symbol of total cleansing, where those baptized promise to henceforth live by God's rules. From the beginning, John the Baptist insisted that they must bring forth the fruits of repentance. (MT 3:1-9; LK 3:8) When one can merely pay a fine for a sin, or be baptized, one may sin with impunity – with the intent to pay the fine or be baptized and commit the sin anyway.

It was common practice for a religion or cult initiation experience to symbolically change the person into something new. Water baptism symbolically erased sins, for example. But to be changed into something new one has to live a changed life, as Jesus and John the Baptist taught.

Muhammad bids us to not be lip service penitents. Repentance has no effect if you continue to do evil, he said.

(S. 4:18) Every soul is held hostage by its own deeds. (S. 74:38) How like the teaching of karma this is! At the time of death everything is sorted out, Muhammad said. (S. 30:14) This is similar to Jesus saying that in the spiritual realm we will be separated like sheep and goats, and wheat and thorns. Though we are automatically judged and come under correction, there is always the opportunity, when we come into materiality again, to choose humility and repentance and thereby mitigate some of the repercussions of law breaking choices we have made in the past.

In Ezekiel (18:5-32) we read that if the wicked renounces all his sins and lives by God's law, he will live and not die, but if the upright abandons his uprightness, all his upright actions will be forgotten. The laws of spiritual nature automatically evaluate each of us by what we do. Shake off all your crimes and make yourself a new spirit, Ezekiel said. Why die (spiritually)? God takes no pleasure in the death of anyone. Repent and keep the law that gives life, he said. (Ezekiel 33:11-16)

Something that might keep us from repentance is judging our Creator. We have to be careful that we don't judge God. Though the way it is phrased in the Bible is that God makes us as He chooses (EX 4:10-12) it is really our past choices and current mission that determine the circumstances and physical condition with which we are born, as well as many of the accidents and diseases that come to us while we are here. The laws that govern spiritual nature are fixed, just like the laws that govern material nature. It isn't God's anger, jealousy or capricious decisions that cause us to suffer, which is the way ancient religions explained pain and suffering. Rather, just as we get hurt when we break a law, or we're involved with someone who breaks a law, that governs in the material realm -- whether we know the law or not -- we get hurt when we break, or we're involved with someone else who breaks, any of the laws that govern the spiritual realm. Rather than judging our

Creator, we should seek to understand what can be learned from our challenges. This is a form of repentance.

God shows faithful love for us by sustaining us here, and working through those who teach us the way to return to being one in purpose with our Creator. (RV 3:12) Our ability to perceive God's love and prepare to reconcile with our Creator begins with repentance.

REPENTANCE EXPERIMENT

If the cells in your body had free will and some chose to be selfish and work against all the other cells, your body would fail to function. Usury is like that. It is an economic system whereby some selfish individuals take money they don't work for and cause imbalance in society.

Where does the extra money come from to pay endless stock dividends and the interest on bonds and savings accounts? It comes, in part, from inflated prices and weakened products – in other words, by sacrificing the health and wealth of those too poor to buy stocks or bonds or to have savings accounts. This is a form of cannibalism.

The usury economic system, which is a form of capitalism, is illogical for several reasons. The usury economic system requires that consumers constantly buy products to keep the economy going, since more money always has to be repaid to the banks than businesses borrow and the government prints. Therefore, products are made to wear out and break quickly so they have to be bought again. This is called planned obsolescence. As a result of this we use more natural resources at a faster rate than the Earth can replenish them, creating imbalances in nature world-wide, and we create more waste than the Earth can process, causing excessive toxic waste that is shipped and dumped, usually in the poorest nations.

For the same reasons – that money is more important than people – some foods are enhanced either with mildly addictive substances and/or with growth hormones to increase sales and consumption. In addition, genetically modified foods are often made using materials never before part of the human diet. Some scientists tell us that they weaken the human immune system, which can make us vulnerable to germs we would otherwise naturally overcome.

It has been revealed in many studies that, after a few people take excessive amounts of money out of the usury driven economic system, wars are necessary in order to infuse large sums of money into the system by employing large numbers of people and using up the expensive disposable product of weapons. (See *War Cycles, Peace Cycles, the necessity for war in modern finance*, by Richard Kelly Hoskins, the Virginia Publishing Company, 1985; *War in the World System*, edited by Richard K. Schaeffer, Emory University, 1988; *A People's History of the United States, 1492-present*, by Howard Zinn, HarperPerennial, 1995; *War, a Cruel Necessity?* Edited by Robert A. Hinde and Helen E. Watson, St. Martin's Press, 1994; *The Best Enemy Money Can Buy*, by Anthony Sutton, Liberty House, 1986; *Phases of Economic Growth, 1850-1973, Kondratieff Waves and Kuznet Swings*, by Solomos Solomou, Cambridge University Press, 1987; *Fuel On Fire, Oil and Politics in Occupied Iraq,* by Greg Muttitt, Random House (in USA by New Press) 2011 and *The Greatest Story Ever Sold, The Decline and Fall of Truth in Bush's America,* by Frank Kelly Rich, Penguin Press, 2006, among many other sources.)

Because of the rules of this game, the rich are able to draw off an excessive amount of money from the system. In order to keep it from collapsing, a war is initiated to give an excuse for the massive infusion of money and to increase employment. (The war of 2003-11 provided money to less developed countries to which U.S. weapons manufacturers sub-contracted. This was to build up their economies so that American businesses could expand in those countries.) But wars also kill people, robbing society of their compassion, insight and contributions, and robbing its victims of opportunities to grow spiritually. Wars destroy families, and ruin cities and the environment.

One side-effect of the United States' unprovoked war against Iraq, and its deliberate poisoning of their land with depleted uranium, is that the persecution of Christians has mushroomed worldwide since 2003. Christianity is the dominant religion in the United States and many U.S. Christians are stockholders. Therefore, Christians worldwide are tainted by association.

Usury breaks the laws against theft and murder, as well as the Golden Rule. It is a subtle system that destroys people and nations as surely as cancer destroys a body. This economic system is illegal according to Biblical Law. God said you shall not lend *anything* on interest. (DT 23:19-21; EX 22:25; LV 25:35-38 and see Ezekiel 18:5-9 and Nehemiah 5:1-13)

It isn't true that, as they say, "capitalism is the worst of all possible economic systems, apart from all the others that have been tried from time to time" -- the standard capitalist justification and mantra. The Maya survived peacefully for centuries without money. The freed Hebrews thrived when they lived by the Biblical law that forbids usury. The current Islamic form of banking is free from the cannibalistic practice of compound interest. What is true is that capitalists actively work to undermine more socially stabilizing systems by using economic and military warfare, and sabotage. They reject and undermine the influences of those who work to shape a stable and harmonious economic environment. And they ignore the needs of those impoverished and damaged physically by their policies. Just like cancer, they eventually kill their host – the country that shaped loose regulations that left a power vacuum for them to exploit.

Muhammad said that Allah has permitted trade, but forbidden usury. (S 2:275) Private ownership of property and businesses is allowed, but laws that encourage unrestricted growth are counter-productive. Usury causes you no increase in heaven. Charity is like bread cast on water – it comes back to you. (S. 30:38) You can't attain righteousness unless you give freely of what you love, he said. What you own is a test. Your highest reward is with Allah. (S. 8:28, 3:92) He also said that riches are fine, but nearness to Allah is the best goal. (S. 3:14 and see 28:60)

Confucius spoke out against competition. He taught that to be secure we should make all secure. (A. 3.7, 6.28) Economically, we should design a system that is cooperative, with the goal of supporting everyone's right to provide for themselves and their family -- instead of one where competition ultimately destroys all in its path, including our health and safety.

There are alternatives to usury. Muslims, for example, have developed a usury free banking system. They charge a set fee for the personal use of money loans and a percent of profit from corporations that borrow money. Islamic interest free banks are available around the world. They are insured, accessible and offer interest free home loans. Interest free banks help create a more stable economic system. There also are barter systems and countertrade, which have been studied and shown to create a more stable economic system. In addition, if governments nationalize their banks then their country doesn't have to pay interest to bankers and do-nothing stock holders. Why make one group of people rich while the whole country is drained of money because of paying interest? Weapons manufacturing should also be nationalized, to take the profits out of war.

Social aids such as food and energy assistance, and aid for the aged and disabled serve to move some money back into society and help stabilize the system, but the greedy rich work to take even this safety net away, believing that they can just move to another country and avoid the consequences (and forgetting that they likely will reincarnate into the consequences -- this is the eternal validity of the Golden Rule). But, in any event, these programs don't solve the biggest problems of usury – war, environmental degradation and poisoned food and water. If we love the way God loves, seeking justice and security for all, we have to choose against easy financial gain for ourselves and in favor of economic and environmental sustainability for all. We must reject usury and return to the economic laws God gave us so Earth can remain a place for souls to incarnate and learn lessons they need to learn to return to God's place.

If we intend to have both national and global societies that are not divided against themselves, we have to change the current economic rules and live by the laws of spiritual nature that forbid murder and theft and that require the Golden Rule. We have to create a sustainable economic system. To know that usury is a form of murder and choose the pursuit of wealth rather than to support a change of system, is greedy. To fail to research the issue of usury and alternative economic models is to craft ignorance. To be too lazy to make the change to a usury free economic model, is sloth. We should repent of using this system, which is forbidden in both the Bible and the Qur'an.

Before their heavy dependence on capitalism, most nations were supported by their farming communities. Weather changes and crop failures drove many off the land and into the arms of industries. Because current economic rules encourage growth and punish sustainability, most industries are susceptible to market saturation. Unless they make weak products and sell to other countries, they risk expanding beyond the capacity of their society to sustain them. A healthier economic system would include tax laws and subsidies that protect the environment, cushion small farms and businesses for years when sales fall off and eliminate do-nothing stock and bond holders and predatory bankers.

A challenging spiritual experiment concerns usury. Those in the developed countries have been raised in a financial environment that includes the usurious form of capitalism and may find it challenging to live without it. But if everyone follows the spiritual laws that govern the acquisition and use of our resources, we can create peace, health and sufficiency. We have the power to do this, but each person needs to do what he or she can if we are going to wrest control over the economy out of the hands of those who depend on businesses that pressure the government to craft laws so they can thrive financially while they destroy our health and the environment.

There is an independent movement worldwide to create a more sustainable economic model. This movement includes:

Islamic style banking – a fee based model of banking without compound interest charges. This form of banking is growing worldwide.

State owned banks, a step away from privately owned banks. Several states are looking at this model of banking, which has been used in some places for over a century. (One reason it is now desirable in the USA is that some states want to launder money from the sale of marijuana, which is illegal (federally) and is counter indicated for public banking.)

Barter and counter trade, classic forms of business and personal exchange.

Crowdfunding – a way to fund projects and start businesses by raising money from a large group of people. Information and several sites are on the Internet.

"Open Source" means sharing intellectual property for free. This practice is growing and includes computer software, medical, pharmaceutical, business and education information. However, a method should be devised to compensate those who make sacrifices in order to research, experiment with, invent and create new information, so that they can continue to add to the free information that enriches us all. Perhaps support can come in the form of government grants or crowd funding for researchers? Wikipedia, the free online encyclopedia used by millions of people, is an example of open source information where donations are requested from the public so they can continue their work.

Sustainable diverse, small organic farms supported by members of the community (Community Supported Agriculture) is another movement that is expanding.

Farm co-operatives, where members live close enough to eat meals together, draw large groups of people back to the land. The Hutterites are an example. Some people in the co-operatives create the machinery needed, some do the book work, others specialize in plant or livestock management or maintain the houses or prepare communal meals.

Fair Trade helps producers in developing countries receive a fair price for their products, and promotes sustainable farming.

Time banks, where people swap services for which they would otherwise pay.

The Center for the Advancement of the Steady State Economy, one of several think tanks where ideas are shared by those seeking a sustainable economy.

Your repentance experiment is to exit the usury economic system as much as possible. Here are some more ideas.

Buy a car you pay for with cash and negotiate for an extended warranty, or use public transit, rather than buying a car on time.

Buy a fixer-upper house you pay for with cash, rather than a new house with a mortgage. Or buy land and build the house piece by piece as you have the money and time.

Don't use a credit card that charges interest.

By way of retirement preparation, consider investing in a business you can participate in part time after retirement and/or property that can be rented or sold after retirement, rather than investing in stocks.

Fund someone else's research or business with an interest free loan.

SPIRITUAL SENSITIVITY

Solomon, a well-known Jewish King, is credited with writing the book of *Ecclesiastes*. He had everything – power, good health, wealth, adulation and hundreds of wives – but in *Ecclesiastes* he shows that he felt that life was empty and vain, just chasing the wind. Why? Because he wasn't growing spiritually. With hundreds of wives, he didn't develop a deep relationship with any one of them. So, he didn't learn how to receive communication from half of God's nature – God's feminine attributes -- because his relationship with women was superficial. Also, since he was too rich and powerful to challenge himself with actions where he might fail and where he would need to ardently seek God's daily guidance, he was coasting through life instead of growing closer to God. His empty feeling was an indication that his spirit was starving for lack of spiritual food.

By contrast, notice that Jesus showed great respect for women -- talking with them, touching them, healing them and teaching them. (John 4:1-42, 8:1-11; Mark 7:24-30; Matthew

8:14-15, 9:25-26, 12:46-50, 15:21-28; Luke 10:38-42) Jesus used the feminine designation for God when he referred to God as the Holy Spirit. He said God is Spirit and wants us to worship in spirit and in truth. He said God will give the Holy Spirit to those who ask for it, and that blasphemy against the Holy Spirit is unforgivable in this life and after. He also highlighted God's feminine side in his teachings. The Hebrews commonly referred to God's masculine attributes of Omnipotent Judge, Enforcer, Protector, Sustainer and Creator. Even though he referred to God as the Father, Jesus taught about God's feminine attributes of Omniscient Comforter, Forgiver, Communicator and Wise Counselor. (Matthew 6:1-6, 16-18. 14-15, 10:16, 12:7; Luke 6:27-38, 11:9-13, 15:4-32; John 6:63, 13:31-35, 14:21, 15:26, 17:23-26)

Jesus taught both that God is Spirit and that in the spiritual realm we do not marry – all is one. (John 4:24; Luke 20:34-36; John 17:21) In Genesis (1:26-27, 5:1-2) it is said that God created them male and female, in the likeness of God. In the wholeness of our spiritual condition we are both male and female. When we come into materiality we choose to accentuate one gender or the other. As an expression of our separation from God we also separate from half of ourselves.

All religions that acknowledge the One God describe God as having both masculine and feminine attributes. God is the Creator, All Powerful Judge, but also the source of Wisdom, Forgiveness and Love. The Abrahamic religions charge us to communicate with God – to listen to God and submit to God's daily guidance. To perceive communications from the full nature of God – the masculine and the feminine attributes – we need to develop respect and listening skills in interacting with both genders in society.

Marriage between a man and a woman is an opportunity to intensely develop respect and spiritual listening skills, as each seeks to meet their separate and combined needs. It is within the security of the committed relationship of marriage that spiritual growth is more naturally developed. Learning how to respect and listen with our spirit to our opposite gender partner helps us develop the ability to perceive and take instruction from God, Who has the attributes of both -- the very goal to which God is leading us throughout the Bible.

In the world there is tension and release, hot and cold, anger and compassion. Without equal opposites there would be either chaos or stagnation. It is opposing forces that both cause and limit movement and growth. Spiritually we need opposites to move us to reflect and to seek with our spirit.

Throughout human history there have been times when societies enjoyed peace and prosperity. Something has always happened to eventually upend that at the personal or the community level. The reason God created Earth was to give us a place where souls that rebelled against Him can learn spiritual lessons and eventually return to submission to our Creator. If we feel too secure with our money or our defense system, then we may be in danger of seeking God less intently. The lack of challenge can trip us up spiritually. We need to keep a spirit that is hungry for God. This was what Jesus meant when he warned that those who love life lose it. We should beware of loving life in this world so much that we risk losing touch with God's Presence and guidance. As we develop spiritual sensitivity, the need for traumatic tensions in our material environment is reduced and we can choose more constructive challenges to which God leads us.

Getting to the point where we are consciously aware of God's Presence and desire to guide us requires spiritual sensitivity. As we grow in spiritual sensitivity we develop the ability to more and more clearly perceive and interpret God's daily guidance.

A unique aspect of the religions that have developed from Abraham's teaching is that we are expected to talk with, listen to and take instruction from the Single Living Designer and Creator of the universe. No other major religion teaches this. In the Bible we are told repeatedly that we are to listen to God's "voice" and obey God. (EX 33:7-11, 19:3-6; DT 26:17, 27:9-10, 28:1-2, 30:19-20; Isaiah 66:3-4; Jeremiah 3:25, 9:12-15)

The teaching that we are to choose God's will over our own was eventually all but lost from Hebrew teaching. Jesus Christ brought it back by word and example. It was then subverted in Christian teaching. Muhammad made it the centerpiece of the Muslim religion. The question that remains is, how do we sensitize ourselves so we can perceive God's communications?

When I was in 4th grade my teacher gave us an assignment to write an essay about what type of career we wanted to work at when we grew up. I couldn't think of anything, so I prayed and asked God what should I be when I grew up. The thought came instantly and powerfully into my mind: "a writer!" What a shock! How could I be a writer? I was just an average student, and I didn't know anything about the writing profession. Besides, hadn't everything that needed to be said already been written? This worried me for years. It was over a decade before I asked God another direct question. I was afraid of what the answer might be!

Humans have always been intrigued by the spiritual side of life and have often sought communication from the spiritual realm, though usually with a buffer instead of by direct listening prayer. Ancient people cast lots, read markings in an animal's liver, or read the way yarrow stalks fell and tried to interpret a response from the spiritual side of life. Hebrews consulted the "urim and thumen," which the Bible doesn't describe. (EX 28:29-30; Nehemiah 7:64-65)

Spiritual communication is real. Moses shared his spirit with the elders of the Hebrew tribes. (NU 11:24-26) The Bible reports that the Witch of En-dor was able to call up the spirit of the prophet Samuel, who was dead, and that he talked with King Saul. (1Samuel 28:10-18) Jesus said that God gives the spirit to those who ask for it. (LK 11:13) There is a report in the Bible that the Holy Spirit came on the disciples at the Feast of Weeks (Pentecost) after Jesus' ascension. (Acts 2:1-4) After Elijah ascended to heaven in a chariot, his servant Elisha took his cloak and gained some of his spiritual powers. Later, a dead man revived on touching the bones of Elisha. (2 Kings 2:9-15, 13:20-21)

Our most important mission while we are in material life is to prepare for our life in the spiritual realm. We are designed to be able to communicate with the Designer and Creator of the universe so we may succeed in our mission.

Sometimes a government has set itself up as if it is beyond criticism or accountability, as if it wants to be the only authority for its people. A government of this type may also refuse its citizens the right to seek God spiritually. This is a violation of two of humanity's inalienable rights. According to the laws of respect – so that one person or group doesn't override the necessary rights of others -- we have the right and the responsibility to seek good governance and to express grievances to our government and work for their peaceful resolution. No human group knows everything about the ever changing world. There must be dialogue and debate so perspectives are shared and needs are met.

In addition, seeking spiritually is what has defined and shaped humanity from the beginning. It's the reason we are here. Seeking spiritually shapes our brain, and our body. It is a natural part of who we are as both spiritual and material beings.

That man does not live by bread alone, but by every word that comes from God, is a consistent message in the Bible. (DT 8:3; MT 4:4; LK 10:38-42) Inspired literature that feeds our spiritual hunger is available in every culture. It helps us to become spiritually sensitive. Becoming spiritually sensitive helps us perceive God's guidance to meet both our material and spiritual needs. If a government tries to force its citizens to focus exclusively on their material needs, the society they create will become unstable because they will be forcing citizens against their spiritual design. To develop spiritual sensitivity is every human's right and purpose, and it should not be denied by a government.

When political leaders do not acknowledge God there is a danger that they also will not want their citizens to seek God. So, while in some countries there isn't a religious test for political leaders, citizens should be aware of the dangers of having leaders who reject God, accountability on the spiritual side of life and the importance of spiritual seeking.

Hindus, Buddhists, Confucians, Jews, Christians and Muslims are alike in many ways, including teaching the seven Fundamental Laws. However, in the matter of how to develop spiritual sensitivity, all are radically different.

Currently Hindus teach that spiritual sensitivity is developed through self-discipline, learning about God as God is expressed in one of the four attributes, working as an instrument of God and worship, praise and adoration for God. According to some Hindu sects, souls eventually become obliterated and merged into God's soul. According to other sects, each soul remains distinct and its union with God is one of love and being in harmony with God.

The Buddha did not acknowledge God. The goal of Buddhism is to overcome all distractions, pains and demands of material life. The opinion is given that, along with a soul group, we have created the illusion of time and substance out of our desires, but then become mired in the complexity of conflicting desires of one another. In order to escape the illusion, at the time of death we must be free of all desires, grudges, egotism and fears. When we are able to overcome all ties to the illusion, we can individually "overcome the world" in ourselves and return to Nirvana –

which is where we came from and is beyond time and substance. A Buddhist monk is taught to daily dispel longing, malice, sloth, distraction and doubt, and to contemplate. The monk's goal is to overcome his sensual desires and his desire for existence. Some Buddhists speak of Nirvana as Power (action) truth (law) eternal, good and their refuge.

Confucius said that it is wise to respect ghosts, but don't seek them. (A. 6.20) He also said that a noble person is in awe of the will of Heaven, and that if you offend Heaven, to whom will you pray. (A. 16.8, 20.3, 17.19) Some claim that Confucianism is more a philosophy or ethics than a religion. However, others point out that it is a way of life that teaches the seven Fundamental Laws, as well as other laws that are also taught by the world's most prominent religions. Confucius acknowledged Heaven, hell and the life of the spirit after death, but refused to speculate on the nature of these or on the nature of a Divine Creator. Spiritual sensitivity, like humanity, is developed through interaction with others and by the self-discipline of living as a "noble" person.

After returning from their painful deportation to Babylon, the Jews were determined to live by God's laws more closely. So, for Jews, the largest of the remaining twelve Hebrew tribes, spiritual sensitivity comes from law keeping. In Deuteronomy (27:26) we are told that anyone who does not live by God's Law (as it was written by Moses) will not experience the Law's confirmation, and they will be cursed. In the Bible, God says to not add to or take away from His Law. (NU 15:30-31; DT 11:1, 10:12-13) Living by the laws Moses was guided by God to write is a spiritual exercise that firms up flabby spirits and signals God and our own souls that we are seeking spiritually. As, step by step, we bring one law after another into our lives, our spiritual senses open more and more to God's presence, power and communication.

Jesus taught the intentions of the Biblical Laws and, after his resurrection, told his followers to go into all the world and teach all nations to obey all that he had taught them. In addition, Jesus taught that God loves every soul. So, for Christians to bring the message of God's love to the world means doing the good deed, giving the kind word, the charitable gift and the brave truth. It means sharing with everyone on Earth, through word and example, Jesus' good news message of God's love and how to return to God's kingdom by loving God and by living a life of accountability. As a result, for Christians, missionary work, community service and the Golden Rule have become the primary ways to develop spiritual sensitivity.

For Muslims, submission to God's guidance, be it for peace or for conflict, is the goal of life. Muhammad said, don't be careless in learning about God, or when trouble comes you will fall away to your detriment. (S. 22:11) Read, study and meditate on the Qur'an. Develop your communication link with the Creator and it will prepare a foundation within you on which to build the ability to become one will with God. Always keep God first in your thoughts and actions.

We can see that spirit food is given in every major religion. But just as no one can build a muscle in your body for you – you must exercise, lift weights and eat nutritious foods yourself – no one can build the muscle or the sensitivity of your spirit. You must feed yourself spiritual food, exercise in prayer and lift the weights of self-discipline.

To rebalance spiritually we must resist the attempts of our inner snakes to draw us back into error with temptations and lies. Secure in God's unending love, we can dare to admit that we are the created who have erred and separated ourselves from our Creator. At peace in the knowledge of God's forgiveness, we can take the steps we need to take to develop spiritual sensitivity. Grounded in experiences of God's presence, we can submit to God's personal guidance for how to change habits of selfishness into habits of trust, obedience and love.

Like water seeks its level, we tend to gravitate to what we most desire, consciously and subconsciously seeking out information and experiences to achieve or acquire it. If your main priority is to have a certain type of body, then you probably will experiment with diet and exercise techniques. You might even have surgery to change your body. If money is your goal, you might study economics, deny yourself and save money, work hard and even justify stealing and cheating in order to reach your goal. If your main priority is to learn the secrets of the spirit, then you will read spiritual literature and experiment with the laws and principles taught there. You might even give up your home or your familiar occupation to pursue a spiritual goal. Abraham did. We all tend to gravitate to our main priority.

When we choose to experiment with the laws that govern the spiritual realm, we grow to understand that a way to reach spiritual goals has been given. One aid in developing this understanding is to keep a daily journal of your experiments with the laws of spiritual nature and evaluate it from time to time. Look for patterns of events that develop in your life that are connected to your experiments.

After we die physically, we will be alive in the spiritual realm where we will be evaluated according to how well we used our time and opportunities while we were on Earth. Developing spiritual sensitivity so we can prepare for that inevitable evaluation, and its aftermath, should be among our highest priorities in life.

Jesus said that what is born of the flesh is flesh; what is born of the spirit is spirit. (JN 3:3-8, 8:31-32) We are going to be reborn in the spiritual realm, and we must prepare a healthy spirit for a successful spiritual rebirth.

SPIRITUAL SENSITIVITY EXPERIMENT

Tithing didn't make it into the Ten Commandments (at least not directly) but it is an intriguing spiritual discipline. Presuming you already keep the Ten Commandments, if you haven't been tithing and you begin giving ten percent of your before tax receipts to your religious organization – to be used to further God's Plan to bring all souls to return to love and submission to God -- you will be surprised how God reveals His presence and power in your life. (GN 14:17-20, 28:20-22; LV 27:30-33)

On the other hand, if you don't give this offering then that money – whether it is saved or spent – is dedicated to something you deem more important than God, which is a form of idol worship. It is idol worship to make anything in your life more important than God, whether it is family, country, comfort or anything else. (EX 20:3-6; 34:12-17) Since idol worship is forbidden in the Ten Commandments, the law to tithe is covered, albeit indirectly.

If you've never tithed, this is a powerful spiritual experiment. Use it for at least twelve weeks. I predict that you won't want to give it up once you try it, though it may require a complete change of lifestyle. When I first started tithing, I found I couldn't afford the house I was renting – so I sub-let it. I had found something much more spiritually satisfying and intriguing. You may not get rich by tithing, but you will gain something more valuable than money can buy.

SUBMISSION TO GOD

In almost every major religion it has become the practice to treat its original teacher like a god – something none of these teachers would have approved. There is more than one reason why people do this. First, we are immersed in material needs, distractions and discomforts, and so we seek a material reference to focus on when we pray. Thus, Hindus create statues to represent attributes of God. Some

Buddhists worship a statue of Buddha. Confucians make sacrifices at temples where he is remembered. It has become popular for some Christians to refer to Jesus as god – conveniently ignoring all his proclamations to the contrary. I have heard Jews say, "Is it good for Israel?" before voting or making financial or other decisions. I have never heard one say, "Is it good for God's Plan to lead all souls on Earth back to being one will with God?" Obsession with a material object, even a country, can blind us to what is eternally valuable to our own soul (and even to the Earth) and can lead us to break the laws that govern spiritual nature in deference to that obsession.

The psychological advantage of setting up a human or a country as a god is that we can then transfer moral responsibility to that person or object and absolve ourselves. "Jesus could live by the Law because he was god," I've heard Christians say. "We are mere humans, so we can't be expected to be so perfect." But God would not give us a burden we are unable to bear, and God said often that the Law is your life. When a young man asked Jesus how to have eternal life, Jesus asked him if he kept the Law.

Like "Adam and Eve" – humankind at its beginning – we still hide God from ourselves out of feelings of guilt, shame and fear of punishment. But like the father of the Prodigal Son, God celebrates every soul that returns in humility, obedience and submission to God. We fear admitting our mistakes. And we are overwhelmed at the thought of the long, exacting journey it would take to fully retrace our steps and undo the damage we have done to ourselves and others. The very idea is daunting. Can't we just say we're honestly, truly sorry and be forgiven? Not exactly.

Jesus shows us that forgiveness and restoration are possible and tells us and shows us how to develop the ability to allow God to lead us to and through opportunities to rebalance spiritually. Once we accept responsibility for where we are – the painful part – and submit to God's guidance – the exhilarating part – we feel hope. We feel washed in God's abundant love. God is for us. We just have to be for ourselves.

No matter how far we have fallen from the mark, God loves every soul and desires that every soul return to oneness with God. Nevertheless, returning isn't instantaneous. We have to prepare a soul that is in sync with the Source of Love and Law. We do that by reversing our habits of choosing self over God and by submitting to God's daily guidance. This requires practice. It requires us to learn from trial and error efforts until we develop the ability to clearly interpret God's guidance. Every human being is capable of doing this. It is what we are designed to do. Though all on Earth have rebelled against their design, all are capable of re-embracing it. Indeed, the opportunity to do so is the very reason for our experience on Earth.

Just look at the grand universe God made as a symbol that God is always with us, caring about us, patiently waiting for us to repent and return. God isn't going anywhere. And wherever our spirit travels in the universe, we will keep experiencing opportunities for spiritual growth until we fulfill our design and return to be of one will with God.

The laws that govern the spiritual realm are fixed and we are not going to return to God's place until we live them for their purpose – to develop spiritual sensitivity so we may perceive and choose God's personal daily guidance to us. It is this second level of obedience – submission to God – that is our ultimate goal and that will bring us to reverse our initial error and prepare us to be reborn humble and contrite into God's place beyond time and substance.

We must meet again our original stumbling blocks, and be able to conquer them. Deep within, each soul knows how it got caught in the material realm: curiosity, lust, revenge, love of power, judging God or something else. The way out is to reverse the way we got in. Know thyself is a mantra that Hindus suggest. Disentangle thine own web, Buddhists would say. Respect the will of Heaven, Confucius taught. Follow God's rules to please God, Jews teach. Live by the way, the truth and life, Christians believe. Submit to God in all things, Muslims tell us.

Muhammad said that God raised him up to create the religion of Islam – submission to God – because this teaching had been almost completely cut out and sublimated in the teachings of the Jews and Christians. Submission to God is the foundation of the Islamic religion, and the ultimate goal of every soul. No one is liberated, at peace, or one with God until they achieve it. Anyone who submits completely to Allah will be rewarded and will be with God, Muhammad said. (S. 2.112)

In the Bible, in Deuteronomy (10:20) we are told to fear God, worship God, cling to God, serve God and swear oaths in God's name. At Sinai, the Hebrews and those with them were told, "You have affirmed this day that the Lord is your God, that you will walk in His ways, that you will observe His laws and commandments and rules, and that you will obey Him." (DT 26:17) In Psalm 143:10 we find one of many references where the psalmist asks God to "teach me to do Your will…"

If Jews practiced submission to God, they would obey God's preference that the place for worship would be centrally located in Israel (at Mt. Gerizim) and that God will designate their leaders from out of all the tribes, not just the Jews. (DT 12:5-7, 27:1-8, 17:14-15) They would end their millennia old grudge holding against Samaritans and their prejudice against Palestinians, Christians, Muslims and all other Gentiles.

In the New Testament Jesus is quoted as saying, "It is not anyone who says to me, 'Lord, Lord,' who will enter the kingdom of Heaven, but the person who does the will of my Father in Heaven." (MT 7:21-27 (TNJB)) When someone

210

said to Jesus, "blessed be the womb that bore you..." he responded, "more blessed be those who hear the word of God and do it." (LK 11:27-28) In the Lord's Prayer he told us to ask for God's will to be done on Earth as it is in Heaven. (MT 6:9-13) God's will can only be done here if we develop spiritual sensitivity, seek to perceive God's will in daily listening prayer, and then do it.

Noah, Abraham, Moses and Jesus were all Islamists. (S. 3:67) They all submitted to God and **taught** submission to God. Muhammad warned, if you live by a religion other than Islam, then when you are in the spiritual realm you will be with those who have lost all that is good. (S. 3:85) All in Heaven and on Earth submit to God's will, he said. (S. 3:83) Don't die except in a state of Islam! (S. 3:102)

SUBMISSION TO GOD EXPERIMENT

Several of the major religions quoted in this book do not require a weekly day of complete rest, when those who have sensitized themselves spiritually through virtuous living turn from the distractions of the world and listen expectantly for guidance from the Living Spirit that designed and created the spiritual and material realms.

Day to day interactions are interrelated and complex. In order to return to submission to our Creator we must develop the ability to perceive God's communications and follow where God leads us to obtain spiritual food and experiences. One aid to developing that ability is to set aside a time when we can empty ourselves of our day to day concerns and open ourselves up to communication from God.

The Bible says that keeping the Sabbath rest is a signal to God that we acknowledge His presence and seek to be obedient to Him. (EX 31:12-13, 17) It is also a signal to our own soul to wake up and become more spiritually sensitive, as we choose by our own free will to take a leap of faith and reach out to our Creator in obedience -- to set our ego aside and to open ourselves up spiritually through rest and reflection for one full day every week. (EX 20:8, 31:12-13, 16-4-17) In addition, when we stop pursuing our desires one day out of every seven, take a step back and open up to God's communications, we find it easier to connect disassociated symbols of order and this helps us develop mentally and spiritually.

The moon has been associated with fertility since ancient times, and crops were planted according to the phases of the moon. Above ground crops were planted when the moon was growing or full, and below ground crops were planted when it was waning or dark. Even today, some farmers plant by the moon's phases. The moon keeps the Earth in orbit and controls water tides, the weather, plant growth and animal fertility. Its four phases are each about seven days long. A lunar month is roughly 28 days. Recognizing this rhythm of seven and honoring it recognizes and honors the One Who created it. (EX 16:1-5, 21-23)

Keeping the Sabbath day holy shows respect and love for the Great Creator, and it shows that we seek to conform to a rhythm made for the world God created – a unique venue where we may repent and prepare to return to our home with God. Parents are pleased when their children show respect for them by following their instructions and giving them attention and affirmation – and God is pleased, too, to have our attention and obedience.

Here is an easy spiritual experiment anyone can use to prove to himself or herself the reality and presence of God. Presuming you are already keeping the rest of the Ten Commandments (EX 20:1-17) to prepare an atmosphere within yourself that will facilitate spiritual discernment – if you haven't been keeping the Sabbath the way the Bible reports that God directed, this is an easy and delightful spiritual experiment through which you can actually experience the presence of the Great Spirit Who designed and created the cosmos.

Keep the Sabbath according to the Bible's rules for the Sabbath for four consecutive weeks. Prepare food in advance so you don't have to cook during that day. Don't require others to work, and don't do any chores or have distractions such as television, computer or telephone. (GN 2:1-3; EX 20:8-11, 16:4-5, 22-23, 29) Begin the Sabbath with trumpet sounds or by singing praises to God. (NU 10:10) Make an offering to God. (DT 16:17) You may attend a religious service. Read the Bible, but not so much that it is work. Sing, pray, meditate, stay in your place and **rest**. Empty your mind and open your spirit to God.

It is traditional at the beginning of the Sabbath to light a candle or an olive oil lamp that will burn for 24 hours. The Spirit of God is described as light (S. 24:35) as is our spirit (Proverbs 20:27). (Many cultures around the world also worship the sun and light, without which there would be no life on Earth.)

Using grains for food and wine for drink is said to have started with Noah after the Great Flood, and blessing these (thanking God for these) may have begun at the same time. (NU 15:17-21) Jesus said to remember him whenever we bless the bread and the wine. (LK 22:19-20) He had already defined his teaching as the bread of life and his example as drink. (JN 6:48-58, 63) So, Christians might use the opportunity of blessing the bread and wine (or "new wine," i.e., grape juice) to remember and recommit to live by Jesus' teachings and example.

If you eat meat, then eating beef, lamb, goat (or some other cloven hooved ruminant) that is free of blood and fat, and abstaining from pork, shellfish and, in addition, all foods that contain artificial ingredients during the four-week experiment, is a way to come closer to what would have been the expected diet at the time the law was written, and will help prepare your mental chemistry for the experiment. (LV 11, 3:17, 2:13)

The reason many Christians worship on Sunday is because that is the day Jesus rose from the dead. For the purpose of this experiment you should keep the Sabbath on the seventh day (Saturday) as the Bible designates. Keep the Sabbath from sundown the "day before" to a little past sundown on the Sabbath. (In Genesis 1 it is said that, "evening came and morning came…" and so forth to count each of the days, indicating that time is counted beginning in the evening.) In the summers you may want to start early so you can eat early, but don't end the Sabbath before a little past sundown.

Keep a daily journal of your thoughts and the events in your life during the four-week experiment, and at the end review it and mark the ways God led you and communicated with you during that time. You will find that as you awaken your soul through obedience, as you reach out to God – Who faithfully waits for just this sign – God will reach back to you with communication and guidance.

This may seem like too easy an experiment. It requires a very manageable amount of self-discipline for a short period of time. Nevertheless, when you use it precisely you will experience its subtle power. If you want to know without a doubt that God is alive, present and concerned about you, you don't have to have a Near Death Experience, just give God the signal God requested through this simple experiment, and analyze the results.

When you have completed the (Ten Commandments and) Sabbath day experiment and recognized God reaching out to begin the process of drawing you back, you will be curious about what other ways God will communicate with you. You can continue your experiments by adding other laws given in the Torah one at a time as you are spiritually guided, and by keeping a journal of the direction and changes that come into your life. Over time you will become a witness to others of the reality of the spiritual realm and of the power, presence and love of its Living Designer and Creator.

THE LAWS

Accountability is a category of laws concerned with spiritual balance.

Reincarnation has to do with the indestructibility of the soul. Its purpose is to provide endless opportunities to achieve soul rehabilitation.

The Golden Rule has to do with the reciprocal effects caused by words and actions.

By practicing endurance, we allow ourselves to be pressured into seeking spiritually. When we respond to stress by seeking spiritual understanding, we show respect to our Creator.

Self-discipline is how we exercise choice to give up some of our power in order to achieve a personal or social goal.

Communication is a category of laws that impact material and spiritual development.

Honesty clears mental and emotional paths to make communication within one's self and in relationships with others easier and more productive. Honesty in communication with God aids our interpretation of God's various ways of communicating with us.

Creativity has to do with the spiritual perception of the intentions of symbols.

Education has to do with the spiritual desire to have better circumstances and meet material and spiritual needs for one's self, as well as the spiritual compassion that draws one to help others have better circumstances and meet their needs as well. Over long periods of time the exercise of learning and teaching has helped develop human physiology and cognition.

Love is a category of laws concerned with actions that are in sync with the Designer Creator Spirit.

Loyalty has to do with taking steps to understand the nature of what we commit to, and then to prepare to keep our promises, help guide and support our loved ones and help guide and support our communal group.

We are a product of order, and design, but we are a product that is conscious of itself -- and that seeks the cause of order. Order is a function of love that gives stability and hope. That we can develop the ability to define and apply the invisible laws of cause and effect order in material nature and in spiritual nature is made possible by spiritual choices that impact our mental ability.

Caution has to do with living by the laws of material nature and spiritual nature, and overcoming temptations caused by pride and material lures, as well as by injustice and tragedy, to learn how to submit to God's guidance. This shows love for ourselves, our family and community, and for God.

Forgiveness has the power to rehabilitate a spirit. It creates an opportunity within one's self and one's social environment to peacefully work out mistakes and misunderstandings and to hold oneself and others accountable in constructive ways.

Expressing joy releases chemicals within us that aid our physical and emotional health, and that encourages our spirit to persevere. It also is a way to show love and thanks to our Creator for the opportunity of material life.

Respect is a category of laws by which the opportunity for spiritual development is protected for ourselves and others.

Respect for human life leads us to seek good physical and social health. By protecting the opportunity for spiritual seeking that we have in this life, we also show respect for our Creator.

Respect for the natural environment leads us to seek good health for the planet. Living sustainably on Earth is another way we show respect for the Creator of the Earth.

Humility has to do with the ability to think and act modestly. This can reduce stress and make it easier to communicate with others, as well as to perceive God's guidance.

In self-defense we protect our opportunity for spiritual growth by protecting our existence on Earth. Sometimes, in self-defense, we may need to surrender money or power so that we may live and continue to learn spiritual lessons.

Daily physical, mental, emotional and relational work shows respect and consideration for others. Because it also builds our mind and spirit, it also shows respect and consideration for ourselves.

Preparing for what comes next is a category of laws by which we prepare for our life as it continues in the spiritual realm after physical death.

Repentance is our portion of the grace equation. God's forgiveness for our errors and guidance for spiritual reconciliation (re-coming) is always available to us, and we perceive and receive it when we humbly acknowledge and take responsibility for our errors and take actions to change in ways that lead us to be one in purpose with our Creator.

Spiritual sensitivity has to do with ways our invisible, ever-living spirit perceives the invisible laws of spiritual nature and receives guidance from the Designer and Creator of the spiritual and material realms.

We are all in "time out" in the material realm because we chose our will over that of our Designer and Creator. Whether we are conscious of it or not, each soul knows that it has turned away from God and that, ultimately, it must turn to and submit to God again. Learning unjudging trust and submission to God is every soul's primary mission. Everything in life is either support for or distraction from that goal, depending on how we respond to it.

THE CHARTS

SEVEN FUNDAMENTAL LAWS OF BEHAVIOR	From the *Egyptian Book of the Dead.* (2345 B.C. but begun long before this date)	Definitions of Hinduism	Quotes of the Buddha From the *Pali Canon*
Do not kill	I have not killed men or women. (4)	To not desire to harm any animal by thought, word or deed is one of the Five Moral Principles.	Don't kill (From the Noble Eight Fold Path)
Do not steal	I have not stolen food (5) or land (17) or anything by force (2)	Prohibition against theft is one of the Five Moral Principles.	Don't steal. (From the Noble Eight Fold Path)
Do not Lie	I have not told lies, closed my ears to truth or exaggerated my words. (8, 11, 31)	Truthfulness is one of the Five Moral Principles that cleanse one of impurities.	Right speech (honesty, no harsh language or frivolous talk.) (From the Noble Eight Fold Path)
Do not commit adultery	I didn't commit adultery.(12)	Control of sexual appetites is one of the Five Moral Principles.	Be free from lust. Don't participate in unlawful sexual conduct. (From the Noble Eight Fold Path)
Be self-disciplined	I didn't disobey the Law (24) nor did I act without due reflection. (29)	One of the Four Paths to achieve liberation from reincarnation is self-discipline.	Right mindfulness (to have positive thinking, to be free from lust, ill-will and cruelty) (From the Noble 8 Fold Path.)
Treat others as you want them to treat you (The Golden Rule)	Egyptians taught reciprocity – that those who helped others could expect to receive help when needed.	The Golden Rule is implicit in the teaching of karma, whereby we receive back words and acts we give to others.	The Buddha accepted the teaching of karma – that we receive back the good and evil that we do to others.
Acknowledgement of the spiritual realm	That they prepared for life after death shows they acknowledged the spiritual realm.	There is a goal to reincarnation. It is to have a last life and stay in the spiritual realm.	The Buddha did not speak of the spiritual realm,. Today Buddhists acknowledge it.

Quotes of Confucius from *The Analects* (A.)	*The Holy Bible King James Version* (Genesis (GN) Exodus (EX) Leviticus (LV) Numbers (NU) Deuteronomy (DT)	Quotes of Jesus from *The Holy Bible King James Version* (Matthew (MT) Mark (MK) Luke (LK) and John (JN))	Quotes of Muhammad from the *Holy Qur'an* (Surahs designated (S))
The one who governs should treat all equally -- don't murder. (A. 20.2)	Thou shalt not kill. (EX 20.13)	Jesus' answer to a man who asked how to have eternal life: Do not kill. (MK 10.19)	God's servants do not commit murder. (S. 25.65-68)
If you gain an advantage, ask yourself if it is fair. (A. 16.10)	Thou shalt not steal. (EX 20.15)	Jesus' answer to a man who asked how to have eternal life: Do not steal. (MK 10.19)	Be honest in financial dealings. Give a just measure and weight.. (S. 11.85)
I don't know how the dishonest manage. A necessary part is missing. (A. 2.22)	Thou shalt not bear false witness against your neighbor. (EX 20.16)	By your words you will be justified and by your words condemned (MT 12.36-37)	Other than truth, there is only error. (S. 10.32)
A noble person doesn't give in to lust. (A. 16.7)	Thou shalt not commit adultery. (EX 20.14)	Jesus sent the woman adulteress, away, called her act a sin, and forbade it. (JN 8.3-11)	Don't commit adultery. It is an evil that leads to other evils. (S. 17.32)
To be fully human, one must control one's self...don't look at, listen to, say or do anything improper. (A. 2.1)	After reminding the Hebrews of God's laws, Moses said, "I set before you life and death, blessing and curse. Choose life." (DT 30.19)	The self-disciplined servant will be rewarded. But the wanton servant will be sent to a terrible place. (MT 24.45-51)	The devil doesn't have any power except our own evil desires. He is only a tempter. (S. 14.22)
One word rule for life? Reciprocity. Don't do to others what you don't want done to you. (A. 15.23)	Love foreigners as yourself, for you were foreigners in Egypt. (LV 19.34)	Jesus said the second most important law is to love your neighbor like your own soul. (MK 12.30-31)	Those who cause good are drawn into good events. Those who cause evil are drawn into evil events. (S. 4.85)
A noble person respects the will of Heaven. (A. 16.8)	Hebrews worship the Invisible Creator of Heaven and Earth, (DT 4.39)	God is Spirit and those who worship must worship Him in spirit and in truth. (JN 4.24)	Those who behave righteously live in delightful gardens in heaven. (S. 68.34)

ACCOUNTABILITY CATEGORY	Egyptian *Book of the Dead*	Definitions of Hinduism	Buddha *Pali Canon*
Reincarnation	Egyptians taught that the soul lives after the body dies, and its evaluation after death determines how it lives in the afterlife.	Words and acts are impressed on the spirit and carry over from life to life.	There is a goal reincarnation aims for, called Nirvana – the end of reincarnation
Golden Rule	Egyptians taught reciprocity – that those who helped others could expect to receive help when needed.	The Golden Rule is implicit in the teaching of karma, whereby we receive back words and actions we give to others.	The Buddha accepted the teaching of karma – that we receive back the good and evil that we do to others.
Endurance		Hindus teach yoga exercises and mental discipline.	Right effort (endure all). (From the Noble Eight Fold Path)
Self-discipline	I have not disobeyed the Law. (24) I have not acted hastily or without due reflection. (29)	One of the Four Paths to achieve liberation from reincarnation is self-discipline. Some sects teach asceticism, to give up certain pleasures to attain spiritual goals.	Right mindfulness (positive thinking, to be free from lust, ill-will and cruelty). (From the Noble Eight Fold Path)

Confucius *Analects*	Bible – Old Testament	Bible – New Testament	Muhammad *Holy Qur'an*
	If a soul is in the farthest part of the spiritual realm and it is time for that soul to return to Earth, God will lead it to that opportunity. (DT 30:4-5 TNJB)	In Luke 1:11-17 an angel informed a priest that a baby (who became John the Baptist) would be born with the spirit and power of Elijah. This had been predicted by Malachi (3:23-34).	Some ask, who will bring us back to life? Say, the One Who created you the first time. (S. 17:51)
One word rule for life? Reciprocity. Don't do to others what you don't want done to you. (A. 15:23)	Love foreigners as yourself, for you were foreigners in Egypt. (LV 19:34)	Jesus said the second most important law is to love your neighbor like your own soul. (MK 12:30-31)	Those who cause good for others are drawn into good events. Those who cause evil are drawn into evil events. (S. 4:85)
A noble person stays steadfast throughout suffering. (A. 15:2)	While wandering in the desert for 40 years the Hebrews were tested with hunger and hardship, yet sustained -- so they would know that the Lord is God. (DT 8:2-6)	Those who endure to the end will be saved. (Matthew 24:13)	There is a great spiritual reward for those who believe, do good works and endure. (S. 28:80)
To be fully human one must control one's self....don't look at, listen to, say or do anything that isn't proper. (A 12:1)	After reminding the Hebrews of God's laws, Moses said, "I set before you life and death, blessing and curse. Choose life." (DT. 30:19)	In a parable, Jesus said that the servant who is self-disciplined and does his job will be rewarded, but the wanton servant will be cut off and sent to a terrible place. (MT 24:45-51)	The devil doesn't have any power except our own evil desires. He is only a tempter. (S. 14:22)

COMMUNICATION CATEGORY	Egyptian *Book of the Dead*	Definitions of Hinduism	Buddha *Pali Canon*
Honesty	I have not told lies (8) or closed my ears to truth. (11) I have not exaggerated my words when speaking. (31)	One of the Five Moral Principles that cleanse us of impurities is truthfulness.	Right speech (honesty and no harsh language or frivolous talk) (From the Noble Eight Fold Path)
Creativity	Ancient Egyptian art and architecture is still studied today.	Dance, music, poetry and literature are of great importance and point beyond the material to heighten spiritual experience.	One of the Buddha's earliest teachings was the widely popular *Book of Eights*, which was thematic poetry he and his followers acted out for audiences.
Education	Egyptian hieroglyphics are among the earliest known forms of writing.	Knowledge/discernment is one of the Four Paths to achieve liberation from the cycle of reincarnation.	The Buddha was a teacher for 45 years. His teachings were spread by his disciples.

Confucius *Analects*	Bible – *Old Testament*	Bible – *New Testament* Jesus quoted	Muhammad *Holy Qur'an*
I don't know how someone who isn't honest manages. A necessary element is missing. (A. 2.22)	You shall not bear false witness against your neighbor. (EX 20:16)	By your words you will be justified and by your words condemned. (MT 12:36–37)	Other than truth there is only error. (S. 10:32)
Poetry builds the mind,. Living virtuously builds character. Music completes the person. (A. 8.8)	Prophets sometimes acted out symbols of God's intentions. (an example at EX 17:8–13)	Jesus' parables used symbols. In the parable about the vineyard, Jesus told the Jews God would give their mission to others because the Jews would kill God's son. (MT 21:33–41)	The Qur'an is a book of poetry so beautiful it has carried the Arabic language over a thousand years.
In China Confucius is known as the Great Teacher. One must love lifelong learning, he said. (A. 17.8)	Teach children the way of the Lord and the Law. (DT 6:4–9, 11:18–21, 32:45–47)	In a parable, Jesus said that those who are lazy and waste the gift of life (by not adding to their learning) will be punished. (MT 25:14–30)	God has chosen you Muslims to be witnesses to mankind. (S. 2:78)

LOVE CATEGORY	Egyptian *Book of the Dead*	Definitions of Hinduism	Buddha *Pali Canon*
Loyalty		The only way to achieve liberation from reincarnation is to complete one of the Four Paths of liberation, which requires loyalty to the disciplines of that path.	The Buddha taught that we should have right intent (focus). (From the Noble Eight Fold Path)
Order	Ma'at (truth/order) was worshipped as a god in Egypt.	Dharma is the sacred truth, or order, that supports the universe, society, religion and personal duty.	The Buddha took problems apart and reconstructed them in logical order to define their intent and value.
Caution	I have not used evil thoughts, words or deeds. (33)		Don't hold opinions one way or another. In this way you avoid heated discussions.
Forgiveness	I have not been exclusively angry. (25)	The concept of karma, the law of inevitable consequences, implies there is value in forgiveness	Don't hold grudges. Clear your mind of grudge holding.
Joy	I have not made anyone cry. (13)	Pleasure is one of the Four Goals humans have.	Buddhists find joy in living without strife, through self-discipline.

Confucius Analects	Bible – Old Testament	Bible – New Testament Jesus quoted	Muhammad Holy Qur'an
The first principle is loyalty. (A. 1.8, 9.25)	In the *Song of Moses* God said He turns away and waits to see what will become of those who are disloyal to Him. (DT 32:19–20)	Jesus said, you cannot be the slave of two masters. You will hate the one and love the other. (MT 6:24)	Regular prayers are required throughout each day to keep God in mind and to remain loyal to God. (S. 17:78)
Confucius said his life goal was to discover the unity that pervades all things. (A. 15.2)	Abraham often defined God as, God Almighty, Maker of Heaven and Earth.	Not one sparrow falls on the ground without God knowing…. Even the hairs on your head are all numbered. (MT 10:29–30)	There isn't anything in Heaven or on Earth that isn't subject to God's command and obedient to His precepts. (S. 30:26)
Those who are cautious rarely err. (A. 4.23, 14.4)	God promised to send a wonder worker who would teach against the Law, as a test to see if we really love God. (DT 13:1–5)	When tempted in the wilderness, Jesus said, "you shall not put the Lord your God to the test." (MT 4:7, quoting DT 6:16)	Be careful that those you befriend don't corrupt you. (S. 3:118) Muhammad also warned that those who don't follow his teachings will be drawn to follow their own lusts. (S. 28:50)
When you see someone who is contrary, look inward and examine yourself. (A. 4,17)	Do not take revenge on your neighbor. (LV 19:18)	If you do not forgive others, God will not forgive you. (MT 6:15 quoting Ecclesiasticus (in the Apocrypha) 28:1–7)	If out of love anyone withholds retaliation, it is atonement for himself. (S. 5:45–47)
To know the truth is not as good as loving it; to love the truth is not as good as delighting in it. (A. 6.18)	Moses said, curses accrue to those who do not serve God joyfully. (DT 28:45–47, 12:11–12)	Jesus attended several celebrations: a wedding, feasts where he taught, the Harvest Festival, the Feast of Dedication (in the winter) and several Passovers.	Muhammad said God told Moses to celebrate His praise with regular prayers. (S. 20:14)

227

RESPECT CATEGORY	Egyptian *Book of the Dead*	Definitions of Hinduism	Buddha *Pali Canon*
Respect for human life	I have not assaulted anyone. (15) I have not behaved with violence. (27)	To practice Ahimsa (to be pure) one should not desire to harm any animal.	The Buddha rejected the caste system and the practice of sati (widow immolation) found in Hinduism. He accepted that both men and women could be his followers.
Respect for the natural environment	I have not polluted the water. (34)	The Earth isn't meant to be a paradise. It is a training ground for the spirit, where we learn spiritual sensitivity and how to become one will with God.	Buddhism teaches that we should not harm any living thing.
Humility	I have not acted with insolence. (41) I have not placed myself on a pedestal. (37)	One of the Five Moral Principles is that to be liberated we must detach from ourselves and become one with what is eternal.	The Buddha and Buddhist monks begged for their daily food.
Self-Defense			The Buddha taught that to be safe we should avoid disputes.
Work	I haven't been power hungry or exceeded my bounds. (30)	One of the Four Paths to liberation from reincarnation is to work as God's instrument – not for money or fame.	The Buddha taught that all should seek right livelihood (i.e., it should be monastic or at least promote life). (From the Noble Eight Fold Path)

Confucius *Analects*	Bible – Old Testament	Bible – New Testament Jesus quoted	Muhammad *Holy Qur'an*
Attend to your own weaknesses instead of condemning others, and put off hostility. (A. 12.21)	Judge all cases fairly for both citizen and resident alien. (EX 23.3, 6; LV 19.15, 24.22; DT 16.20, 1.16–17)	If you love only those who love you, what good is that? Be perfect, as your Father in Heaven is perfect. (MT 5.44–48)	Repel evil with good. Seek God's guidance when incited to quarrel. (S. 23.96, 41.36)
The noble person doesn't compete with others…(A. 3.7) To be secure, make all secure. (A. 6.28)	Agriculture laws are found at Leviticus 18.19, 22.6–7, 24–28, 23.10–11, 25.1–12; and Deuteronomy 20.19–20, 22.9–10, 25.4	Jesus said that those not trustworthy with money won't receive what is their very own, meaning spiritual skills and strengths. This warning applies to our relationship with Earth's resources as well. (LK 16.10–13)	Muhammad said, let business be with mutual good will and don't waste your profits. (S. 7.31)
If you would have respect, be righteous and humble. (A. 12.20)	Be God's servant on Earth. (DT 10.12)	No one comes to heaven without being as humble as a little child. (MT 18.1–4)	There isn't anyone who is alive in Heaven or on Earth but must be God's servant. (S. 19.93)
A noble person, being virtuous, has no anxiety, being wise, is not perplexed, and being courageous, has no fear. (A. 14.30)	We are responsible for our own lives as well as the lives of others. (GN 9.5)	Because a time of crisis was imminent, Jesus said, "now….if you have no sword, sell your cloak and buy one." (LK 22.36)	Defend yourself if you are attacked unjustly. (S. 26.227)
Choose a job you love and you'll never have to work a day in your life., is a saying attributed to Confucius.	Work for six days each week. (EX 20.19)	Teach all nations to obey everything I have commanded you. (MT 28.20)	If you are doing work God guides you to do, don't worry about anyone who mocks you…. (S. 7.42)

PREPARE FOR WHAT COMES NEXT	Egyptian *Book of the Dead*	Definitions of Hinduism	Buddha *Pali Canon*
Repentance		Some Hindus teach that one may be able to repent in this life by following the guidance of a priest to live righteously and give charitably.	By teaching change and a more disciplined life, the Buddha taught repentance.
Spiritual Sensitivity	I have not committed evil. (32) I have not sinned. (1)	God-seeking is the search for meaning and value in life, beyond self-centeredness.	The Buddha taught right concentration (yoga for meditation) (From the Noble Eight Fold Path)
Submission to God		To work as God's instrument is one of the four paths to liberation from reincarnation.	

Confucius *Analects*	Bible – Old Testament	Bible – New Testament Jesus quoted	Muhammad *Holy Qur'an*
By drawing out our inner nobility and encouraging changing to a virtuous life, Confucius taught the concept of repentance.	Ezekiel said, why die? God takes no pleasure in the death of anyone. Repent and keep the law. That gives life. (EZ 33:11-16)	*After* his resurrection, Jesus told his disciples to go to all nations and teach repentance for the forgiveness of sins. (LK 24:45-48)	If those who have sinned repent, pray regularly and give charity regularly they should be accepted into the faith. (S. 9:11)
A noble person guards against lust, argumentativeness and excessive acquisition. (A. 16.8)	Anyone who does not live by God's law will not experience the law's confirmation, and they will be cursed. (DT 27:26)	Jesus said that only those who do God's will can understand his words, (JN 8:43-47) and that if you live by his teachings, you will know the truth and the truth will set you free. (JN 8:31-32)	Pray before sunrise, after sunset and at the sides of the day. (S. 20:130)
A noble person respects the will of Heaven. (A. 16.8)	God commands us to seek communication with Him and to heed His specific guidance to us. (EX 19:3-6; DT 26:16-17)	Jesus said he was facing the crucifixion so the world would see his submission to God. (JN 14:30-31) And he told us to imitate him. (JN 15:1-6)	Anyone who lives by a religion other than Islam (submission to God) won't be accepted by God. (S. 3:85)

Bibliography

50 Simple Things You Can Do To Save Earth, edited by John, Sophie and Jesse Javna, Hyperion Books, 2008

A Handbook of Native American Herbs, by Alma R. Hutchins, Shambhala Publications, Inc., 1992

Agenda For A New Economy, From Phantom Wealth to Real Wealth, by David C. Korten, Berrett-Koehler Publishers, Inc., 2009

Air Pollution and Non-Communicable Diseases, A Review by the Forum of International Respiratory Societies' Environmental Committee, Dr. Dean E. Schraufnagel, et. al, World Health Organization, 2018

Ancient Religions, Edited by Sarah Iles Johnston, The Belknap Press of Harvard University – Press, 2007

An English Interpretation of The Holy Qur'an with full Arabic text, by Abdullah Yusuf Ali, Bilal Books, 1996

An Inconvenient Truth, by Al Gore, Rodale press, 2006

A People's History of the United States, 1492-present, by Howard Zinn, HarperPerennial, 1995

A Philosophical Framework for Rethinking Theoretical Economics and Philosophy of Economics, by Gustavo Marques, World Economics Association Books, 2016

Are EDC's Blurring Issues of Gender? by Ernie Hood, Environ Health Perspect, January 2006, 114(i): A21 (EDC/endocrine disruptive chemicals)

Assessment of the Effects of Barter, International Trade Commission, 1985

Beyond Growth: The Economics of Sustainable Development, by Herman Daly, Ph.D., Beacon Press, 1996 (and see the website for Steady State Economics)

Booker T. Whatley's Handbook On How to Make $100,000 Farming 25 Acres, by Booker T. Whatley and Editors of New Farm, Regenerative Agriculture Association, 1987

Born Again: Reincarnation Cases Involving Evidence of Past Lives, With Xenoglossy Cases Researched by Ian Stevenson, M.D., by Walter Semkiw, M.D. 2011

Chaos: Making a New Science, by James Gleick, Viking Penguin, Inc., 1987

Children and Television: A Global Perspective, by Dafna Lemish Malden, MA, Blackwell Publishing, 2007

Confucius,The Analects, translated by James Legge, Introduction by Lionel Giles, Digireads.com Publishing, 2017

Confucius, The Analects, by Raymond Dawson, Oxford University Press, 2008

Collapse of a fish population after exposure to synthetic estrogen, Karen A. Kidd, Paul J. Blanchfield, Kenneth H. Mills, Vince P. Palace, Robert E. Evans, James M. Lazorchuk and Robert W. Flick, *PNAS* (Proceedings of the National Academy of Sciences of the United States of America) March 29, 2007

Confucius and Confucianism – Questions and Answers, by Thomas Hoguck Kang, Ph.D., Confucian Publications, 1997

Cradle to Cradle, by William McDonough and Michael Braungert, North Point Press, 2002

Criminological Theory Past to Present, edited by Francis T. Cullen and Robert Agnew, Roxbury Publishing Company, 1999

Darwin's Unfinished Symphony, How Culture Made the Human Mind , by Kevin LaLand, Princeton University Press, 2017

Deep Ecology for the Twenty First Century, edited by George Sessions, Shambhala, 1995

Defense Spending and Economic Growth, by James E. Payne and Anandi P. Sahn, Editors, Westview Press, 1993

Desert Mirage: The True Story of the Gulf War, by Martin Yant, Prometheus Books, 1991

Did Our Species Evolve in Subdivided Populations across Africa, and Why Does It Matter? by Scerri, E.M.L., Thomas, M.G., Manica, A., Gunz, P., Stock, J., Stringer, C.B., Grove, M., Groucutt, H.S., Timmermann A., Rightmire, G.P., d'Errico, F., Tryon, C., Drake, N.A., Brooks, A., Dennell, R., Durbin, R., Henn, B., Lee-Thorpe, J., deMenocal, P., Petraglia, M.D., Thompson, J., A., Scally, A., Chikhi, L., *Trends in Ecology & Evolution* 33, 582-594.

Diet For A Small Planet, by Frances Moore Lappé, Small Planet Institute, 1985

Do GMOs Accumulate Formaldehyde and Disrupt Molecular Systems Equilibria? Systems Biology May Provide Answers by V. A. Shiva Ayyadurai, Prabhakar Deonikar; Histochem, *Cell Biology* (2008) 130:967–977

Easy Green Living: The Ultimate Guide to Simple, Eco- Friendly Choices for You and Your Home, by Renee Loux, Rodale, 2008

Eco-Economy, Building an Economy for the Earth, by Lester R. Brown, W.W. Norton & Company, New York London, 2001

Ecological Literacy, Education and the Transition to a Postmodern World, by David W. Orr, SUNY series in Constructive Postmodern Thought

Ecological Literacy, Educating Our Children for a Sustainable World, edited by Michael K. Stone and Zenobia Barlow, Sierra Club Books, San Francisco, 2005

Edgar Cayce's Story of Jesus, by Jeffrey Furst, The Berkely Publishing Group, 1976

Egyptian Book Of The Dead, originally translated by Karl Richard Lepsius, 1842, also translated by E.A. Wallis Budge

Estrogen in birth control diminishes sex organs in male rats, by E. Mathews, T.D. Braden, C.S. Williams, J.W. Williams, O. Bolden-Tiller and H.O. Goyal, *Environmental Health News,* January 15, 2010

Exploring Reincarnation: The Classic Guide to the Evidence for Past Life Experience, by Hans TenDem, Arkana, 1990

Finance As Warfare, by Michael Hudson, World Economics Association Books and College Publications, 2015

Fish Devastated by Sex Changing Chemicals in Municipal Wastewater, by Dr. Karen Kidd, University of New Brunswick and the Canadian River Institute, 2008

For the Common Good: Redirecting the Economy Toward Community, the Environment and a Sustainable Future, by Herman Daly, Ph.D. and John B. Cobb, Jr., PhD, Beacon Press, 1994

FoxFire, edited by Eliot Wigginton, Doubleday & Co., 1972-2015, (this is a series of 12 books that carry Foxfire in their title. The subject is Appalachia and sustainable early American crafts and skills)

Fuel On Fire, Oil and Politics in Occupied Iraq, by Greg Muttitt, Random House (in USA by New Press) 2011

Getting Us Into War, by Porter Edward Sargent, P. Sargent, 1941

Give and Take, a Revolutionary Approach to Success, by Adam Grant, Viking (the Penguin Group) 2013

Groundwork of the Metaphysics of Morals, by Immanuel Kant, 1785

Harmonica, by Ptolemy

Holy Bible, Authorized The King James Version, World Bible Publishers, Inc.

Holy Bible From the Ancient Eastern Text, George M. Lamsa's Translation from the Aramaic of the Peshitta, HarperSanFrancisco, 1933 and 1968

Hutterite Beginnings: Communitarian Experiments During the Reformation, by Werner O. Packull, The Johns Hopkins University Press, 1999

Identifying and Harvesting Edible and Medicinal Plants in Wild (and not so wild) Places, by Steve Brill, with Evelyn Dean, HarperCollins Publisher, 1994

Inventing Reality: The Politics of News Media, by Michael Parenti, St. Martin's Press, 1993

JPS Hebrew-English Tanakh, The Traditional Hebrew Text and the New JPS Translation – Second Edition, The Jewish Publication Society, 1999

Larousse World Mythology, edited by Pierre Grimal, translated by Patricia Beardsworth, The Hamlyn Publishing Group, Limited in USA, by Excalibar Books (Simon & Schuster) 1965

Life After Life, by Raymond Moody, M.D., Mockingbird Books, 1975

Long term toxicity of a Roundup herbicide and a Roundup-tolerant genetically modified maize, by Gilles-Eric Séralini, Emilie Clair, Robin Mesnage, Steeve Gress, Nicolas Defarge, Manuela Malatesta, Didier Hennequin, Joël Spiroux de Vendômois, *Food and Chemical Toxicology* 2011 May 31(4):528-33.

Longitudinal Relations Between Children's Exposure to TV Violence and Their Aggressive and Violent Behavior in Young Adulthood: 1977-1992, by L. Rowell Huesmann, Jessica Moise-Titus, Cheryl-Lynn Podolski and Leonard D. Eron, University of Michigan, American Psychological Association, Inc., 2003, vol 39 No. 201-221

Maternal and fetal exposure to pesticides associated to genetically modified foods in Eastern Townships of Quebec, Canada, by Aris Leblanc; *Journal of Hematology & Thromboembolic Diseases --* ISSN:JHTD, an open access journal   Volume 1 • Issue 1 • 100-104, 2011

Measuring the Correlates of War, by J. David Singer and Paul F. Diehl, University of Michigan Press, 1990

Megamedia Shakeout, by Kevin Maney, John Wiley & Sons, Inc., 1995

Molecules of Emotion: The Science Behind Body-Mind Medicine, by Candace Pert, Ph.D., Touchstone, 1997

Nanoparticles – A Thoracic Toxicology Perspective, by Rodger Duffin, Nicholas L. Mills and Ken Donaldson, Yonsie Medical Journal, August 2007

Neurosciences: From Molecule to Behavior – a university textbook, by C. Giovanni Golizia and Pierre-Marie Liedo, Springer Spektrum, Berlin, Heidelberg, 2013

No More Throwaway People: The Coproduction Imperative, by Edgar Cohn, Essential Books, 2000

Only One Earth, the care and maintenance of a small planet, by Barbara Ward and René Dubos, W.W. Norton & Company, Inc., New York, 1972

On the Origins of War and the Preservation of Peace, by Donald Kagan, Doubleday, 1995

Optiks, by Isaac Newton

Other Lives, Other Selves: A Jungian Psychotherapist Discovers Past Lives, by Roger J. Woolger, Ph.D., Bantam Books, 1988

Our Stolen Future, by Theo Colborn, Dianne Dumanoski and John Peterson Myers, Dutton, 1996

Phases of Economic Growth, 1850-1973, Kondratieff Waves and Kuznet Swings, by Solomos Solomou, Cambridge University Press, 1987

Plan B, by Lester R. Brown (founder of World Watch Institute; see that website for his books written from 1963-2015. There are several books in the Plan B series)

Plastic: A Toxic Love Story, by Susan Freinkel, Harcourt

Plastic Free: How I Kicked the Plastic Habit, by Beth Terry, Skyhorse Publishing, 2015

Post-Capitalism: A Guide To Our Future, by Paul Mason, London Penguin Books, 2016

Prenatal Exposure to Diethyistilbestrol (DES) in Males and Gender-Related Disorders: Results from a 5-Year Study, by Scott P. Kerlin, Ph.D..DES Sons International Network, International Behavioral Development Symposium 2005, in Minot, North Dakota

Prosperity Without Growth: Economics for a Finite Planet, by Tim Jackson, Abingdon, Oxon, 2017

Rig Veda, a compilation of ancient Hindu religious songs and sayings

Scapegoats: a Defense of Kimmel and Short at Pearl Harbor, by Edward L. Beach, Naval Institute Press, 1995

Science and Human Values, by Dr. Jacob Bronowski, Harper Torchbooks, The Science Library Harper Row Publishers, 1956

Scientific American Special Issue: The Science of Being Human – Humans: Why We're Unlike Any Other Species on the Planet, Editor-in-Chief Mariette DiChristina, September 2018

Scientists: harmful hormones from birth control pills can't be filtered out in sewage treatment, by Thaddeus Baklinski, *LifeSiteNews,* September 12 2012

Sexually Dimorphic Non reproductive Behaviors as Indicators of Endocrine Disruption, by Dr. Bernard Weiss, Environmental Health Perspectives, 110 Suppl 3, 387-91, July 2002

Silent Spring, by Rachel Carson, Houghton Mifflin Company Boston, 1960

Small Business For Dummies, by Eric Tyson and Jim Schell, John Wiley & Sons, 2008

Steady State Economics, by Herman Daly, Ph.D., Island Press, 1991

Streetwise: Race, Class and Change in an Urban Community, by Elijah Anderson, The University of Chicago Press, 1990

Steering Business Toward Sustainability, by Fritjof Capra and Gunter Pauli, United Nations University Press, 1995

The Analects of Confucius, translated by Simon Leys, W.W. Norton & Company, Inc., copyright by Pierre Ryckmans, 1997

The Best Enemy Money Can Buy, by Anthony Sutton, Liberty House, 1986

The Book of Eights, attributed to Gautama Siddhartha

The Buddha before Buddhism: Wisdom from the early teachings, by Gil Fronsdal, Shambhala, 2016

The Compendium of Music, by Rene Descartes

The Creator and the Cosmos: How the Latest Scientific Discoveries of the Century Reveal God, by Hugh Ross, Ph.D., Nav Press Publishing Group, 1993

The Doctrine Of The Upanisads And The Early Buddha, translated by Shridhor B. Shrotri, Motilal Banasidass Publishers, Pvt. Ltd., Delhi, 1951

The Everything Green Living Book, by Diane Gow McDilda, Adams Media, F+W Publications, 2007

The Gnostic Gospels, by Elaine Pagels, Vintage Books, A division of Random House, 1981

The Greatest Story Ever Sold, The Decline and Fall of Truth in Bush's America, by Frank Kelly Rich, Penguin Press, 2006

The Harmony of the World and Music of the Spheres, by Johannes Kepler

The Herb Book, by John Lust, N.D., D.B.M., Bantam Books, 1974

The Historical Dictionary of Hinduism, New Edition, by Jeffery D. Long, The Scarecrow Press, Inc., subsidiary of The Rowman & Littlefield Publishing Group, Inc., 2011

The Hutterites in North America, by Rod Janzen and Max Stanton, The Johns Hopkins University Press, 2010

The *Interlinear Greek-English New Testament, with lexicon by George Ricker Berry,* Baker Books, a Division of Baker, Book House Co., Twenty-Second printing, 1999

The Interpreter's Bible, Abingdon Press, 1952

The New Jerusalem Bible, Doubleday & Company, Inc., 1985 edition.

The Pharmacopedia of the People's Republic of China, by the China Food and Drug Administration, 2015, usp.org

The Physiology of Mind-Body Interactions, by Gregg D. Jacobs, Ph.D., Journal of Alternative and Complementary Medicine, Vol. 7, Supplement 1, 2001, pp 83-92

The President's War: The Story of the Tonkin Gulf Resolution and How the Nation Was Trapped in Vietnam, by Anthony Austin, Lippincott, 1971

The Religion And Philosophy Of The Veda And Upanishads, by Arthur Berriedale Keith, Greenwood Press, Publishers, 1925 and 1971

The Vietnam Wars 1945-1990, by Marilyn B. Young, Harper Collins, 1991

The Wheel of Life: A Memoir of Living and Dying, by Elisabeth Kubler-Ross, M.D., Touchstone (Simon & Schuster, Inc.) 1997

The Word of the Buddha, from the Pali canon, translated by Nyanatiloka Mahathera, Colombo, 1927

The World's Religions, A Guide To Our Wisdom Traditions, by Houston Smith, HarperSanFrancisco, a Division of HarperCollinsPublishers, 1991

This is Your Brain on Music: the science of a human obsession, by Daniel J. Levitin, a Plume book (Penguin Group) 2007

'Til There Was You, by Meredith Wilson for the 1957 play, "Music Man."

Time Dollars: The New Currency that Enables Americans to Turn Their Hidden Resource – Time – into Personal Security and Community Renewal, by Edgar Cohn, Rodale, 1992

Total War: Causes and Courses of the Second World War, by Peter Calvocoressi and Guy Wint, Penguin Press, 1972

Truth is the First Casualty: The Gulf of Tonkin Affair: Illusion and Reality, by Joseph C. Goulden, Rand McNally, 1969

Upanisads, translated by T.M.P. Mahadevan, Published by Arnold Heinemann, 1975

War, a Cruel Necessity? Edited by Robert A. Hinde and Helen E. Watson, St. Martin's Press, 1994

War Cycles, Peace Cycles, the necessity for war in modern finance, by Richard Kelly Hoskins, the Virginia Publishing Company, 1985

War in the World System, edited by Richard K. Schaeffer, Emory University, 1988

Where Reincarnation and Biology Intersect, by Ian Stevenson, M.D., Praeger Publishers, 1997

Why Your Child is Hyperactive, by Ben Feingold, M.D., Random House, 1974

Made in the USA
Columbia, SC
19 April 2021